W9-BNZ-633

Sources of Difference in School Achievement

Alan Brimer, George F. Madaus,
Bernard Chapman, Thomas Kellaghan and
Robert Wood

NFER Publishing Company

Published by the NFER Publishing Company Ltd.,
Darville House, 2 Oxford Road East,
Windsor, Berks. SL4 1DF
Registered Office: The Mere, Upton Park, Slough, Berks. SL1 2DQ.
First published 1978
©Alan Brimer, George F. Madaus, Bernard Chapman, Thomas Kellaghan
and Robert Wood
Limp edition ISBN 0 85633 155 4
Hardback edition ISBN 0 85633 168 6

Typeset by Jubal Multiwrite Ltd., 66 Loampit Vale, London SE13 7SN
Printed in Great Britain by
Page Bros. (Norwich) Limited
Distributed in the USA by Humanities Press Inc.,
Atlantic Highlands, New Jersey 07716 USA.

Contents

B
29.5
G7
567

Introduction

While the publication of the report on the Equality of Educational Opportunity Survey (EEOS) (Coleman *et al*, 1966) and the controversy which followed it provoked the study reported in this book, the occasion for it was the common concern of the researchers in the USA, England and Ireland over the consequences of the report's reception for educational policies. England seemed an appropriate country in which to re-examine some of the issues raised by the EEOS findings; not only does that country possess convenient vestiges of institutionalized, privileged education, but it has also established a tradition of questioning in official reports (Robbins, Plowden) the social justice of state education and of seeking the remedies for social inequality in the re-organization of schools and the supplementation of their resources.

The expectation of those who began the EEOS was that differences would be found to exist between schools in the south and north of the United States and particularly between negro and white schools in such matters as quality of staff, school buildings, equipment, libraries and per capita expenditure. After this had been demonstrated, it was believed that equality could be achieved by Federal Aid programmes. At the time, many people believed that educational, 'inputs' or the 'quality of the schools' as measured in the conventional terms of the EEOS rigorously determined the level of academic achievement in them. In fact, the difference between inputs turned out to be quite small and, while there were differences in facilities which positively related to academic achievement, these were much less than had been expected.

The fact that the EEOS failed to demonstrate that differences in educational achievement can be attributed to differences in school provision has been variously interpreted, but undoubtedly the survey was not designed for this purpose and the statistical analyses applied were less relevantly focussed on such questions than they might have been. Dissatisfaction with the EEOS led to the particular questions to which the present enquiry was addressed.

Our study addressed itself to four main issues. Firstly, are the contributions of schools — their curricula, their resources, their organization, their teaching — to differences in achievement greater than those suggested by the EEOS, when examinations focussed on prescribed curricula replace objective tests of academic aptitude as the criterion measures?

Secondly, when the sample of students studied is more homogeneous in level of educational survival than that in the EEOS, are school and teacher effects more in evidence? A major problem in interpreting the results of the EEOS is that the whole range of individual differences in achievement of students had been used to determine whether schools made a difference. Given an amount of variance constituted in this way, by far the greater part of it was likely to arise from individual and family sources and, since differences between schools are not so monotonously distributed, the proportion of the variance they contributed would be both small and unrevealing. In order to detect whether schools make a difference it seems more reasonable to constitute a sample of children who are less heterogeneous with respect to their achievement up to the point at which achievement was being assessed.

Thirdly, when the unique contributions to achievement variance of families, individuals, schools and teachers are separated from the contributions they make in common, does the family influence loom so large as would be expected from the EEOS?

And fourthly, if indicators of school, individual and teacher attributes are replaced by measures of the processes, attitudes, and values of the agents, do such measures increase the explanatory power of the independent variables?

The authors, members of research teams in the three countries, cooperated in preparing a proposal to the Carnegie Corporation which was submitted in 1973 on behalf of Boston College and the study was subcontracted to the University of Bristol in January 1974. The design of the study required that the sample be drawn from a set of students, all following the same prescribed curricula, taking the same examinations, at a level at which pre-selection on the basis of achievement would have reduced individual variation in the ability to follow the curricula. These students were to be drawn from schools which varied in their provision and in their overall academic orientation. The O (Ordinary) and A (Advanced) levels of the General Certificate of Education (GCE) examination were chosen as satisfying the curricula and examination conditions and as being taken by students surviving into the academic section of the fifth and seventh years respectively of secondary school in England.

It is evident that the intention of the study was not to generalize its conclusions to the population of school children in England, but to set a target population defined by candidates for a public examination who were in schools of different types. While the sample did not prejudice the study in favour of school rather than of family associated variables, it nevertheless increased the likelihood that if differences in achievement, associated with school variables, did exist, they would be detected.

The London University Schools' Examination Council agreed to make available the marks of candidates for the summer examination in 1974, provided that the schools concerned agreed. Agreement of schools was in the last resort less important than the agreement of the Local Education Authorities administering the schools. In the end, four Local Authorities (three 'Home Counties' and one London Borough), which had a preponderence of schools with candidates for University of London examinations, agreed to take part. Questionnaires to be completed by candidates, by their teachers and by school principals were constructed and piloted by April 1974 and were administered in the collaborating schools in May 1974. Nationally collected data, documenting the characteristics of the participating schools, were made available by the Local Education Authorities. Examinations were taken in the summer of 1974.

It was decided to carry out analyses separately in terms of each of the separate subject examinations taken at O and A levels. Thus, univariate and bi-variate values differed for many variables from subject to subject. For example, teacher variables frequently reflected only those teachers involved in teaching the subject which was a dependent variable to the examination candidates under consideration. Following trial analyses using total variance, a decision was made to run separate analyses on between- and within-school data in order to avoid confusion over the proportion of explained variance allocated within schools and the proportion allocated between schools. The strategy adopted was first to identify five blocks of variables, which were named School, Teacher, Family, Individual and School-Individual blocks. The last of these arose from some of the process variables in which pupils were asked to respond to questions on their evaluation of the school, which, for the between-schools analyses were presented as combinations of pupil perception and school characteristics. The precaution was taken in assigning pupil variables to blocks for the separate analysis of within- and between-school variance to use school means for the between-school analyses and to use deviations from school means for the within-school analyses.

Each of the blocks of variables was considered to be capable of making a unique contribution to explained variance. In the first stage of the analysis, all variables within each block were entered into a regression analysis and achievement regressed on them. The resulting regression coefficients were considered for each subject separately and the independent variable was retained for future analyses involving that subject if the coefficient was significantly different from zero. At the second stage, achievement was regressed on the surviving variables in each block and subsequently on all possible combinations of the five blocks. By solving a series of simultaneous equations, it was possible to determine from the results of the regression analyses the proportion of variance ascribable uniquely to a block and that which it explained in common with other blocks. The particular virtue of this approach is that it requires no *a priori* decision as to the order in which blocks are entered into the regression analyses, nor does it leave the proportion of variance ascribed to blocks to arise merely from the precedence with which intercorrelations of the variables suggest that the explained variance can be maximized at any given stage of addition of variables.

For example, family-associated variables may be expected to have effects before the child enters school but also to continue to have an effect after the child has entered school. Indeed, they may affect the school to which the child goes, as well as being affected themselves by the child's achievement in the school. Similarly, while the overt material resources of schools can be separately identified, schools as institutions are much more than the aggregate of physical resources. It is the interaction between school facilities and policies, the qualities of the teachers and the student body which contribute to the organic entity which is a school. By using the technique of symmetric variance decomposition, it was possible to give due weight to the contribution of the blocks. Insofar as the explanation of achievement variance is shared by a number of blocks, priority is no longer assigned to the block which has the highest overall contribution to variance. A major disadvantage of the technique was the extensive computing that was required. There were 32 regression analyses for the between-school runs and eight for the within-school runs for each subject. In all, for the 11 O-level subjects and four A-level subjects, this step involved 600 regression analyses.

It has been a common feature of similar studies that the proportion of criterion variance identified as being between schools is small. In the present study, the between-school variance was less than 20 per cent of total variance in only two of the 11 O-level subjects and two of the four A-level subjects. In three of the O-levels and one of the A-levels, it exceeded 30 per cent. The total variance explained by all five blocks was higher than one generally encounters. In only two of the O-level subjects and in none of the A-level subjects was less than 40 per cent of total variance explained. In five of the O-levels and two of the A-levels, more than 50 per cent of the variance was explained. Nevertheless, in common with other studies, more of the between-variance was explained than of the within-school variance. In general, almost all the between-school variance could be accounted for, as against about one-third of the within-school variance.

The results displayed a surprising degree of uniformity across subjects. In both O and A-level subjects, while almost all the explained within-school variance was accounted for by the Individual block uniquely, substantial unique explanation of between-school variance was confined mainly to the School and Teacher blocks. Most of the between-school variance was shared amongst all blocks, although it is worth noting that Teacher or School blocks had the highest shared contribution in seven of the O and three of the A-level subjects. In only one of the subjects did the Family block achieve this status. This uniformity of results was remarkable insofar as it was achieved despite marked differences in the constitution of the subject samples to which our report necessarily draws attention.

In interpreting the results, it must be remembered that the sample was deliberately selected to be homogeneous in that the children concerned had already been pre-selected as O-level candidates. A further point that must be borne in mind is that the social class composition of the school was included as a school variable and that there were significant social-class differences between schools. Only for a small subsample, too small to be informative, were initial ability levels of children at the time of their entry to school available. The results are interpreted as implying a collusive effect of family background and individual ability upon admission to schools which had better facilities and better qualified and more experienced teachers and which led to superior achievement. It is seen to be a consequence of a collusive, societal process, which is most likely to culminate and cohere in the type of school attended. The results are seen as in general supporting, although expanding and amplifying, the most comparable piece of earlier research done in England some ten years previously (Pidgeon, 1967).

The main difference between the results of our study and those of the EEOS is that differences in achievement are seen, not as being uninfluenced by school factors, nor as being a monotonous result of an inexorable family background, but rather as consequences of progressive differentiation. It could be said that schools mobilize the best of their resources to maximize the best that each student has to offer and, that in doing so, schools are properly adaptive. Alternatively, it might be argued that schools maximize differences between pupils as a substitute for the adaptations required to give each pupil equal status. Whichever interpretation is adopted, this study suggests that schools do make a difference, in concert with other societal agencies, and that they are responsive to the same trends to which these other agencies are subject and which the society as a whole adopts. Perhaps the expectation that schools can counter the trends of society is false, but it is this expectation that leads to the sense of disillusionment when schools are shown not to compensate for the ill-effect of the practical rules by which society governs its progress.

The authors wish to express their appreciation to the Carnegie Corporation of New York for providing financial support for the study.

Many people gave generously of their time, advice and services either in the planning of the study, during its execution or in its preparation for publication. For assistance at various stages of the project, we wish to thank Chris Amos, Ernest Rakow, Fritz Mosher, Peter Airasian, David Cohen, Henry Acland, Carolyn Ferguson, George Hudson and B.K. Passi. We are indebted to Mary Rohan who was responsible for the preparation of the manuscript, to Patricia Kingston who typed it, and to Mairead Byrne for bibliographic assistance. We wish to acknowledge the cooperation of the Department of Education and Science, Local Education Authorities and the headmasters, teachers and students of the participating schools. To all of the above we wish to express our gratitude.

List of Tables and Figures

Chapter One

The Study of School Effectiveness

A large number of investigations of the working of formal educational systems, or parts of them, has been carried out since the inception of mass education and particularly during the course of the present century. Studies have focussed on a variety of phenomena and have adopted varying approaches. In some of these, school systems have been examined only in terms of input variables (*e.g.*, quality of teachers, availability of libraries, laboratories and aids, teacher-pupil ratio), though presumably, it was assumed that such variables are functional in terms of school output measures, such as student achievement. In other studies attempts have been made to monitor a school system over a period of time in terms of output, without necessarily attempting to relate such output to input factors. Recent examples of studies of this kind are those of reading standards of pupils in Britain (Start and Wells, 1972) and the more wide-ranging National Assessment of Educational Progress studies in the United States (National Assessment of Educational Progress, 1974).

In a final category of investigation, and it is this type that is of most interest to us here, school input measures have been explicitly related to measures of school outcome. In studies of this kind which were carried out during the first half of the century, various aspects of schooling — cost, size of school, size of class, organization of the school, method of teaching, amount of time given to instruction and attendance — have been related to various measures of school achievement (*cf.* Stephens, 1933; 1967). On the whole, the results of the studies underline what Stephens (1967) has called 'the constancy of the school's accomplishment' (p. 71); the relationship between achievement and individual school factors has at best been modest.

Three points may be made about these studies. Firstly, the criterion of school effectiveness was most commonly scholastic achievement, as measured by norm-referenced, standardized tests. Secondly, most studies were based on univariate analyses, although some did attempt to control for factors such as intelligence and the background of students. And thirdly, the vast majority of the studies were survey or quasi-experimental in design. All three factors limit the value of the studies in attempting to answer questions about the effectiveness of schools.

In the past 20 years, the 'revolution of competence' in the computer world has meant that investigators are no longer limited to the inclusion of a small number of variables in analyses, thus overcoming one of the disadvantages of earlier studies. The feasibility of large-scale complex investigations has been reflected in the number of multivariate studies of school effectiveness which has been carried out since 1956 — most of them since 1960 (*cf.* Averch, Carroll, Donaldson, Kiesling, and Pincus, 1972). On the whole, however, studies of school effectiveness have continued to use norm-referenced, standardized tests of achievement as measures of school output and, with some exceptions which have attempted a more experimental approach, have also continued to be of the survey type.

Nevertheless, by the mid-1960s the character of studies of school effectiveness was changing in ways other than their size. In particular, the impetus and rationale for such studies were changing. Such investigations would no longer be left solely to the initiative or resources of researchers. For a variety of reasons, the interest of government agencies in the questions of school effectiveness and of educational reform increased and, as a consequence, such agencies became directly involved in the commissioning and execution of empirical investigations. This involvement led to investigations which had among their aims the resolution of policy issues (*cf.* Cohen, 1970). The first major empirical investigation of the American school system undertaken in the interests of the policy formation of the United States' Government was commissioned in 1964 and reported two years later (Coleman, Campbell, Hobson, McPartland, Mood, Weinfeld, and York, 1966). At the same time, a similar survey with rather similar purposes — though at the elementary level only — was carried out in the United Kingdom (Great Britain: Department of Education and Science, 1967).

It is of interest that both these studies were concerned with the concept of equality of educational opportunity. Coleman *et al* (1966), in both the title of their report (*Equality of Educational Opportunity*) and in outlining the rationale of their study, clearly indicated that they were concerned with educational opportunity, particularly in the context of children of ethnic and racial minority groups. The concept of equality of opportunity is not a new one, though its interpretation has changed over time. Traditionally, it has been felt that equality of opportunity existed if free schools and exposure to a given curriculum are provided, in other words, if all children — irrespective of creed, colour, class, sex or financial resources — have equal access to educational facilities (Coleman, 1968). Reflection on the basic concept of educational equality, together with a number of social and legal developments, have given rise in recent years to several new and more radical definitions of the term. These have not led to general agreement on meaning, however, and recently, Coleman (1975b) has indicated that we have now come to the point where we must question the value of continuing to use the term. For his study of *Equality of Educational Opportunity* (Coleman *et al.*, 1966) however, he accepted five possible interpretations of the term and hoped that the study would cast light on all five. These five interpretations referred to differences in the community's input to the school (*e.g.,* per-pupil expenditure, school plants), racial composition of the school, intangible characteristics of the school (teacher morale and expectations), equality of results given the same input of pupils, and equality of results given different inputs of pupils (Coleman, 1968). One of the major virtues of the study, according to Coleman (1972), was to shift policy attention from its traditional focus on comparisons of inputs to a focus on output and the effect of various inputs on output.

Studies of school effectiveness

In attempting to throw light on equality of opportunity (in its many meanings) in American schools, Coleman *et al.*, (1966) focussed on three major areas of investigation: a description of resource inputs of elementary and secondary schools, a description of levels of achievement in grades 1, 3, 6, 9 and 12 of students in schools, and an analysis of the effects of various inputs on achievement. The overall findings of the study have been the subject of considerable publicity. Firstly, while schools attended by minority pupils tended to have poorer physical and programme facilities, the differences in input between schools attended by minority and white students was not as

great as had often been assumed. Secondly, with some exceptions – particularly Oriental Americans – the average minority pupil
scored lower on standardized tests of ability and attainment than the
average white pupil. Thirdly, within-school variance in attainment was
found to be much greater than between-school variance. For example,
for twelfth grade northern whites, only 8.25 per cent of the total
variance was between schools. Finally, facilities and curricula of schools
were found to account for relatively little variation in pupil
achievement. It is this finding that has received most subsequent
attention. Its implications were spelled out in the report:

> . . . schools bring little influence to bear on a child's achievement
> that is independent of his background and general social
> context; . . . this very lack of an independent effect means that
> the inequalities imposed on children by their home, neighbour-
> hood, and peer environment are carried along to become the
> inequalities with which they confront adult life at the end of
> school. For equality of educational opportunity through the
> schools must imply a strong effect of schools that is independent
> of the child's immediate social environment, and that strong
> independent effect is not present in American schools (Coleman
> *et al.*, 1966, p. 325).

The results were not quite as expected. Coleman's own expectation
had been that the survey would find large differences in facilities
between schools attended by negro children and those attended by
white children (Mosteller and Moynihan, 1972). Furthermore, much
educational practice is based on the belief that facilities are related to
school achievement. The findings that school characteristics alone
accounted for a relatively small proportion of variance in achievement
was taken to indicate 'that professional practice in a major social
institution was not nearly so efficacious as had been thought'
(Moynihan, 1968). Such a conclusion was hardly likely to be welcome
in the educational establishment.

Reactions to the report were in fact varied and critical. Criticisms
ranged from political ones that perceived the findings as 'near-racist'
(*cf*. Moynihan, 1968) to technical ones, relating to procedural and
mechanical errors in handling data (Smith, 1972), non-response and
selective participation (Hanushek and Kain, 1972; Jencks, 1972b) and
to possible defects in the report's method of analysis. It is perhaps this

last point that has received most attention. It has been pointed out that carrying out separate analyses for regional and ethnic groups reduces heterogeneity in schooling and achievement, thus reducing the likelihood of finding relationships (Dyer, 1968). On the other hand, it has been pointed out that Coleman *et al.'s* failure to distinguish between different kinds of high schools (trade, vocational, academic and comprehensive) in their analyses might have led to a confounding of factors relating to school achievement and student self-selection (Smith, 1972). Finally, it has been argued that the regression model used in the study underestimated the role of school resources, since school factors were introduced into the analysis only after student background factors had been 'controlled' (Smith, 1972; Wiley, 1976).

Actually, the results of the Coleman survey should not have come as a surprise to people familiar with the findings of other studies which had examined the relationship between school facilities and achievement. We have already noted that early univariate studies did not reveal consistent and significant relationships between any school variables and achievement. More recent multivariate studies provide basically similar results (*e.g.*, Benson *et al.*, 1965; Burkhead, Fox and Holland, 1967; Goodman, 1959; Kiesling, 1969; Mollenkopf and Melville, 1956; Peaker, 1967; Sohlman, 1971). But somehow the Coleman report brought home to the educational community in a way which earlier studies had not done how unimportant variations in many school facilities might be.

The richness of the Coleman data, together with the impact of the study on the educational community, led to a number of re-analyses of the data. Smith (1972) carried out re-analyses with subsamples of northern students at the sixth, ninth and twelfth grade levels, in the light of errors in, and criticisms of, the original study. In particular, he questioned Coleman's model of the educational process and choice of statistics. The Coleman approach assumed that five sets of variables or factors determine a student's achievement: home background, characteristics of student body, the school's facilities and curriculum, his teacher's characteristics and other unmeasured factors of his heredity and environment. Furthermore, the five factors were treated in the analyses as if they were additive, and on the assumption that background factors operate prior to school experience, the former were entered in regression equations before the school factors. As Smith points out, this has the effect of assigning to home background factors the explanatory power which they share with school resources as well as the explanatory power they possess uniquely.

This problem was attended to in more recent analyses of the Coleman data carried out by Mayeske and his colleagues (Mayeske, Wisler, Beaton, Weinfeld, Cohen, Okada, Proshek and Tabler, 1972; Mayeske, Okada, Cohen, Beaton and Wisler, 1973). In these analyses, a symmetric variance decomposition method was employed which allowed the relationship between school factors and student achievement to be shown without first allocating all of the shared variance to the home background of the student. Unique contributions of variables to variance as well as common contributions of sets of variables can be estimated using this method.

Despite differences in approach, more recent re-analyses of the Coleman data have been interpreted as basically confirming the original findings. This is true up to a point. In Smith's (1972) re-analyses, a very large amount of school-to-school variation in achievement was attributable to differences in home background, actually more than in the Coleman analyses (over 66 per cent for white secondary students and about 33 per cent for black students) and the relationship between school resources and verbal achievement was found to be very slight. In the re-analyses of Mayeske *et al.*, (1972), as well as using the symmetric variance decomposition technique, modifications were also made to the Coleman data. In particular, the criterion measure of school outcome used was an overall achievement composite based on a factor analysis of five measures (general information, reading comprehension, verbal ability, mathematics achievement and non-verbal ability) rather than the single measure of verbal ability used for the most part in the original Coleman study. Using the composite measure of achievement, greater between-school variance was found than in the Coleman analyses. For example, for a twelfth grade sample, 34 per cent of the total variance in the composite measure was associated with the school students attend; the figure for ninth grade students was 37 per cent. Furthermore, such variance was attributable mainly to home and school factors acting in concert rather than to home factors operating uniquely.

The studies we have considered were all carried out in the United States. The findings of a large-scale study at the elementary level in Britain are not basically dissimilar. These show that variation in parental attitudes account for more of the variation in children's school achievement (measured by performance on a standardized test of reading comprehension) than either variation in the material circumstances of the home or variation in schools (Peaker, 1967). Several studies in Europe also show that school factors explain less variation in test scores than do social background factors (Sohlman, 1971).

At an international level, the investigations of the International Association for the Evaluation of Educational Achievement (IEA) have been studying educational achievement in a variety of subject areas (mathematics, science, reading comprehension, literature, civic education, French as a foreign language and English as a foreign language) across 21 countries. The research had as its aim the identification of the factors accounting for differences between countries, between schools and between students (Postlethwaite, 1975). Achievement tests, which it was hoped would be suitable in all countries, were specially constructed for the projects. On the whole, the method of construction seems to have followed normal psychometric procedures, though every effort was made to sample all behaviours and contents appearing in the original table of specifications (Comber and Keeves, 1973; Husen, 1967; Lewis and Massad, 1975; Purves, 1973; Thorndike, 1973). Using a regression model in which home background factors were entered first (as had been done in the EEOS study), it was found that the average contribution of home background variables to total variance in between-student analyses ranged from one to 29 per cent for 14 year old students; the average for science, reading comprehension, literature, French reading and English reading was about 15 per cent. Previous schooling (type of school and/or type of programme) showed a greater range – from zero to 52 per cent. On average, it contributed less to the explanation of between-student variance than home background. The average contribution of 'learning conditions' (amount of prior instruction, characteristics of teachers) was similar to that of previous schooling (Postlethwaite, 1975).

Quite large differences were found between countries in the relationship between attainment on the one hand and home and school variables on the other, as Postlethwaite (1975) points out. For example, when home background was aggregated to the school level (neighbourhood effect), it accounted for 80 per cent of between-school variance in science achievement in Scotland, while in Sweden the figure was only eight per cent. Conversely, school factors made a large contribution to variance in achievement in Sweden, but not in Scotland. As an explanation, it is suggested that school neighbourhoods are more homogenous in Scotland than in Sweden. Whatever the explanation, it is clear that conclusions about the contributions of home and school factors to achievement which are based on studies which have been carried out within one country, where variance in any of the independent variables may be limited, may be misleading.

One IEA study stands out as being particularly relevant to the present investigation. This was a study of the mathematical attainments of British school children (Pidgeon, 1967). It is of particular interest since the sample for the study was chosen to be representative of secondary school students in England and Wales, and so, it provides a point of reference, some ten years earlier, for the present investigation. It is also of interest because the British educational system at the secondary level provides on the one hand a greater variety in school provision and, on the other hand, because of its selectivity, greater homogeneity in student characteristics than does the American educational system. Given these differences in the educational systems of the two countries, it is of interest to compare the findings of the IEA study in Britain with the results of studies which have been carried out in the United States.

The criterion measures in Pidgeon's study were tests of mathematical attainment and, since these were restricted to those agreed as part of the international study, they were not directly equivalent to GCE O-level examinations. Nevertheless, the follow-up data that are reported suggest that the mathematics scores obtained were substantially correlated with subsequent achievement in O-level examinations. The sample was drawn from secondary schools in England and Wales and was stratified by type of school. The students were candidates for various GCE O-level board examinations, amongst which there were some from the London Board. Additional questions were incorporated into the questionnaires for the national study which were not part of the international enquiry and these questions served to make the English study peculiarly fitted to the characteristic structure of English education.

The O-level sample was made up of 3,466 students drawn from 157 schools. Because of the expectation that type of school would prove to be an important variable, schools in the population were first stratified by type before random sampling within strata began. The importance of school type as it applies to the present investigation can be judged from the data reported by Pidgeon (1967, Table 3.3) in describing his sample; from the data differences in resources of types of school are apparent. For example, for Direct Grant and Independent Schools, the ratio of specialized mathematics teachers to pupils is 1 : 141; for Grammar schools, it is 1 : 178; for Comprehensive schools, 1 : 221; and for Modern schools 1 : 296. Thus the positively selective Direct Grant, Independent and Grammar schools were specially privileged in the provision of specialized teachers in mathematics. Likewise, the per-pupil expenditure on teachers' salaries expressed the more general nature of privilege in teacher provision. In other sections of Pidgeon's report (Pidgeon, 1967, Table 3.10), it is revealed that more of the teachers in the positively selective schools had received university training in the subject matter that they taught — over 70 per cent in the positively selective schools, and under 60 per cent in the remainder. Strangely, however, a higher proportion of teachers in the selective schools than in the remainder considered the student to be more important than the subject being taught. Figures are also reported for the A-level sample where the differences are in the same direction and in some cases even more striking. The general background of the pupils in each of the school types displays the inherent bias amongst the O-level candidates attending the positively selective schools.

It is evident that children taking O-levels in the positively selective schools are somewhat younger than the remainder, are more likely to have fathers in higher occupational groups, mothers who do not work and who themselves received a positively selective education. The same general trend is true of the A-level candidates.

The results on the mathematics tests did not, however, present a uniform picture of the association between possession of privileged resources and family background, and higher attainment. Students in Direct Grant and Independent schools, that represent the highest level of privilege, do not achieve the highest mean score, which is achieved by students in Grammar schools, and even do somewhat less well than students in Technical schools (Pidgeon, 1967, Table 4.4). A likely explanation lies in the academic selection of children. Although in the competitive eleven-plus examinations, children at the top of the list were normally allocated to Grammar schools, in those cases where Technical schools were available, such places were offered to pupils whose academic assessment fell just below that which would have given them a grammar school place.

The method of analysis adopted in Pidgeon's study was to divide variables into four blocks, namely, sex and age, family, type of school, and school variables; then, having subjected all variables to a conventional multiple regression analysis, selected blocks of variables were partialled out and the proportion of the explained variance attributable to the blocks at each stage was observed. No division of variance into within and between school components was attempted. The results for the first stage of analysis appear to indicate that 'schools' have the largest effect, being associated with 14.8 per cent of assignable variation, even after 'type of school' has been allowed for, and that 'family' variables have the smallest effect (.06 per cent of assignable variation) (Pidgeon, 1967, Table 8.3). Even when one of the variables in the school block, the social class level of the school, was moved from that block to the family block, the effect was to increase the percentage of variation assignable to the 'family' block to only 3.3 and to reduce that for 'school' to 12.1.

Commenting on the behaviour of the family variables in the various analyses applied to populations ranging from 13-year olds up to A-level candidates, Pidgeon (1967) notes that

> . . . the family contribution to the assignable variation becomes steadily less as the amount of selection increases. For population 3a (A-level candidates) it is negligible. This is because the ablest children of parents at the lower end of the occupational scale are still at school by this stage.
>
> This effect of progressive selection was well marked in the international enquiry. It is only in the United States that the parental variables were still important at the 3a stage. This is because the proportion of the population still at school at the age of 17 is far larger and less selective in the United States than elsewhere (p. 219).

The findings of this study again serve to underline the danger of drawing general conclusions about school effectiveness from studies restricted to one country, where variance in any of the independent variables considered may be very limited.

School inputs

Even in investigations carried out in the United States, there are considerable differences between studies in the independent or predictor variables employed. This, of course, makes comparisons between studies difficult, though it may also be interpreted as making the similarity of findings regarding the role of the school all the more impressive. However, it could also be that all the studies are defective in some way in their choice of independent measures. For example, there has been a strong emphasis on the use of status variables (*e.g.*, size, volumes per pupil in school library) rather than on process or psychological ones in describing the school and the home (*cf.* Coleman *et al.*, 1966; Jencks *et al.*, 1972; Mayeske *et al.*, 1972), despite evidence that measures of process are likely to show stronger associations with student learning than measures of status, whether one is speaking of the home (Bloom, 1964) or of the school (Dyer, 1968; Jencks, 1972a). We are reminded by Rivlin (1971) that 'the number of volumes in the library is presumably not as crucial as the choice of books and their accessibility' (p. 75). On the basis of the limited evidence available to date, it seems likely that research that attends to the activities and climates of schools rather than to their static characteristics will be more successful in identifying school-based variables which are functional in student achievement.

School outputs

Just as problems in the measurement of independent variables create difficulty in the interpretation of studies of school effectiveness, so do problems in the measurement of dependent variables, *i.e.*, the measures of school outcome. These problems range from the philosophical to the technical. The problems are philosophical in that they touch on issues related to the purpose of schooling. Studies of school effectiveness have not concerned themselves with such issues, however. In most such studies, the focus of concern has been cognitive development. This may be because it is easier to assess development in this area than in say the sphere of social or emotional development, or it may be because cognitive factors seem important in the public mind; they are emphasized in examinations and much of the recent criticism of schools has been, not that schools do not foster emotional or social development, but that children leaving them cannot read or write (Kellaghan, 1977).

Not only has cognitive development been the focus of most studies of school effectiveness, but invariably it has been measured by means of a standardized norm-referenced test (Cohen, 1972). This we saw was true in the case of the IEA studies as it was of the EEOS study (Coleman *et al.*, 1966) and its re-analyses (Mayeske *et al.*, 1972; Smith, 1972). Jencks (1972b) has drawn attention to the fact that school achievement as measured by the Coleman tests in fact measured only one dimension of achievement. A principal components factor analysis showed that the first principal component accounted for between 92 and 96 per cent of the variance at different grades. The highest loading in each case on this component was achieved by verbal ability measures. In other words, it was the verbal ability nature of the tests that defined the variability used to represent differences in achievement.

It is not difficult to understand why standardized tests of ability and achievement have been selected as the criterion variables in studies of school and programme effectiveness; the tests had a perceived validity, good psychometric rationale and a history unmatched by any other measurement technique. Indeed, the extent to which the use of such tests had become ingrained in American culture can be seen in the fact that most criticism concerning the use of standardized tests in programme evaluation and policy research studies has been directed towards the issue of the extent to which the behaviours included in such tests represent the full range of behaviours fostered by the school. Until recently, little criticism has been directed at other aspects of these tests (Carver, 1974; Coleman, 1975a; McClelland, 1973; Porter and McDaniels, 1974). Rather, critics appear to have accepted the psychometric adequacy of standardized tests as measures in assessing the differential effects of schooling, calling for basically similar instruments to assess a broader range of school outcomes. The prospects in other areas of measurement, however, have not seemed very promising. Furthermore, there is, on the face of it, no reason to believe that non-cognitive outcomes, such as attitudes, interests and values are more susceptible to differences in school resources than they are to home background factors (Madaus and Linnan, 1973). In fact, it is probable that basic cognitive skills are more easily taught than are non-cognitive ones. Hence, if we are unable to find relationships between school resources and achievement, it would appear that small refuge can be taken in the fact that higher level cognitive and affective outcomes have been omitted in most studies.

If we confine ourselves to the measurement of the cognitive outcomes of schools, can we be satisfied that standardized tests, as they exist, are the most appropriate instruments? A consideration of the character of standardized tests prompts us to suggest that we cannot. The effect of a sophisticated technology of test development has led to routine ways of constructing tests, irrespective of whether these are measures of ability or of achievement. Following the introduction of behavioural measures of intelligence, group measures of human abilities were developed in which the main concern was to create instruments which were homogeneous with respect to the construct being assessed, reliable, valid in that they did indeed represent the construct, and discriminating in that they maximized the individual differences amongst any given population for which they were intended. The same techniques and criteria were ultimately employed in developing measures of achievement. However, certain reservations began to be recognized concerning the relevance of these criteria to tests reflecting school curricula. Increasingly, the internal consistency of the questions of a test with one another, which was achieved by selecting items for which the intercorrelation with others was high, led to a purging of questions which demanded specific knowledge. In particular, the use of estimates of reliability, depending upon internal consistency, led to an over-emphasis on a general factor, which in terms of school achievement is normally verbal and numerical ability.

Likewise, the use of multiple-choice questions, with their considerable advantage of administrative convenience, contributed to the over-generalization. A multiple-choice question invites a choice of one from a number of possible answers. The difficulty of a question can be varied by making the choice more or less complex. Nevertheless, a question contributes most to discrimination between able and less able students if approximately half get it right. Therefore, test construction favours the selection of questions at a middle level of difficulty. The wrong answers are then inserted, not as inert place holders for those who do not know the answer, but with the intention of catching out the student who can only partially solve the question. Consequently, it is difficult for the less able student to demonstrate how much he does know, since the little he is able to contribute is carefully engineered to make him appear to be wrong. Using the criteria by which the tests were judged, they appeared to be working quite satisfactorily, yet their real effect was to make differences between children, particularly children in the same school, appear to be greater than they really were; and because the tests had been engineered through their homogeneity to exclude specific knowledge, they under-represented the contributions that different schools, through their differences in curricula, made to differences in achievement.

Even after Bloom (1956) revolutionized the techniques of curriculum evaluation, following the publication of his Taxonomy of Educational Objectives, tests continued to be built in exactly the same way. Thus the massive studies conducted by the IEA (Comber and Keeves, 1973; Purves, 1973; Thorndike, 1973), with some exceptions, came to conclusions very similar to those of Coleman *et al.* (1966) but used tests constructed in this same manner. The implication of the foregoing would seem to be clear. If we are to measure achievement appropriately, then we must examine the achievement that schools themselves seek, that is achievement in which the curriculum is adequately reflected.

Methods of analysis

A final problem in the measurement of school effectiveness is the appropriateness of the method of analysis used to examine the relationship between student, school and home factors on the one hand and school achievement on the other. The most common technique used to analyze data collected to examine school effectiveness in large-scale surveys has been multiple regression, a technique which attempts to analyze the collective and separate contributions of two or more independent or regressor variables to the variation in a dependent variable (Kerlinger and Pedhazur, 1973). The dependent variable, in studies of school effectiveness, has of course been some measure of output, nearly always as we have seen, a measure derived from performance on a standardized test of ability or achievement. The regressor or independent variables have been various input measures such as indices of students' home background, teacher characteristics and school facilities.

Problems in the use of regression analysis occur when one is dealing with a large number of independent variables which are intercorrelated among themselves, which seems to be the case for variables included in studies of school effectiveness. Two issues have received attention in the context of this problem. One has concerned the selection and grouping of variables for use in analysis and the other has concerned the order of the entry of the variables into the analysis. The problem of grouping has been dealt with in several studies by the 'blocking' of variables which are conceptually similar to each other and which exhibit certain empirical relationships (*e.g.*, significant partial correlation coefficients with a given number of dependent variables). In general, blocks are constructed to represent home background factors on the one hand and school factors on the other. In the final regression analyses in which the relationship between independent variables and school output is examined, the variables which survive to represent blocks are entered as blocks rather than being allowed to compete with all other variables.

In the EEOS and IEA studies, the home background was entered first in analyses, on the assumption that 'since the student's background is clearly prior to, and independent of, any influence from school factors, these background factors can and should be held constant in studying the effects of school variables' (Coleman *et al.*, 1966, p. 330). This procedure has the obvious disadvantage of assigning to the family background block both the explanatory power which it possesses uniquely and the explanatory power which it shares with the other blocks. To overcome problems associated with this approach, a method of symmetric variance decomposition has been suggested (Beaton, 1973, 1974; Mayeske *et al.*, 1972; Wisler, 1974). Its purpose is to partition 'explainable variance in a dependent variable into the portions attributable to each independent variable and to all combinations of independent variables in order that we may better understand the interactions of predictors in estimating the criteria' (Beaton, 1974, p. 63). In this approach, the partitioning of variance is not dependent on the order in which variables are entered. Thus, for example, no *a priori* decision is taken to assign to the home, variance which is jointly attributable to home and school factors.

Obviously, the relationships between home, school and achievement, which studies of the effects of schools have set out to explore, are extremely complex and present a challenge to the analyst. It seems unreasonable to expect that all achievement variance should be explained by school factors, when school is taken to mean the attributes of the school after the effects of individual differences among students have been controlled. Schools are corporate institutions and it is the student-body, the teacher-body and school characteristics that contribute to any effect produced. Without the specific characteristics of any of these, a school would be unrecognizable as such.

In the asymmetric variance decomposition techniques used in the IEA studies and that of Coleman *et al.* (1966), we saw that home background was entered first into the regression analysis because of the chronological priority that was attached to the home background of the child. The effect of this procedure is to reduce very considerably the possibility of school effects being demonstrated. Yet it is apparent that home background is not a variable which ceases to have an effect at the time at which a child enters school; rather, it is one that continues to exercise an effect throughout the school career of the student. We must begin to ask what effect home background should be expected to have apart from the initial readiness for school that it pre-empts. Modern educational thinking emphasizes the desirability, even the necessity, of the school working in close affiliation with the home, and curricula are moving closer to the conception of locally based and locally relevant fields of study. It is, therefore, likely that in contemporary educational practice we will find school characteristics closely related to the characteristics of the student-body and the local environment. In this situation, between-school variance in output measures should inevitably be affected by the commonality between the school and its environment.

It should not surprise us then if studies of schooling find that the commonality of student block variables and school variables is large. We are aware that differences between schools in achievement are a function of the selectivity of schools as well as of their differential effect. We are aware, also, that within schools, differences in achievement are a function not only of differential teaching and curricula but also of the scholastic aptitude, aspirations and motivations of the students, all of which are related to their home background. Blocks of variables are conceptual entities; they abstract from real life by grouping together those variables which logically fit the classes of explanatory variables that we have chosen to use. Viewed in this way, commonalities between blocks are not evidence of unintended excessive collinearity: they are essential ingredients of our explanations of a dynamic system which has been reduced to a set of static observations.

Conclusion

In conclusion, we may consider briefly the contribution of the studies we have considered to our knowledge of the effectiveness of schools. Firstly, the large-scale surveys which have been carried out (*e.g.*, Coleman *et al.*, 1966; Mayeske *et al.*, 1972, 1973; Postlethwaite, 1975; Smith, 1972) tell us nothing about the absolute effects of schooling; that is, we are not able to say on the basis of such studies whether or not children benefit by attending school. There is some other evidence, however — historical and quasi-experimental — that suggests that the cognitive and scholastic skills of children who do not attend school are inferior to those of children who do attend (Madaus, Airasian and Kellaghan, in press).

Secondly, large-scale surveys do not clearly indicate the relative importance of background and school factors for a student's attainment. The frequently cited conclusion that the home is a much more potent influence than the school in affecting attainment has to be treated with caution in the light of problems associated with the choice of independent and dependent measures and with methods of analysis of data. On the last point, when analyses permit the common as well as the unique contributions of variables to be demonstrated, the common influence of the school and the student's background is found to exceed either of their distinguishable influences (Mayeske *et al.*, 1972). Given the reality of the interaction between the home and the school, it would perhaps be surprising if one could identify large unique contributions of either institution.

Finally, little can be said on the basis of existing studies about the differential impact of schools. While most large-scale studies indicate that variations in the inputs of schools do not seem to have much effect on student performance, we are again faced with problems of interpretation because of possible lack of variance in school variables as compared to background variables and because of the nature of the predictor and criterion variables employed. As far as variance in school and background variables is concerned, there is some evidence that inferences based on the Coleman data may not be telling the whole story. Studies carried out in countries other than the United States, where a greater variety of school provision is coupled with greater homogeneity in the student body, suggest that school factors may be more important than the American studies indicate.

These conclusions about the findings of studies of school effectiveness may seem rather tentative and may be taken to lend support to the view that the direct contribution of research to the improvement or modification of social programmes — including educational ones — has at best been marginal (*cf.* Bidwell, 1973; Cohen and Garet, 1975; Ornstein and Berlin, 1975; Rossi, 1972; Weiss, 1973). Certainly, research to date has not discovered any consistent and significant relationships between individual school characteristics and achievement. This is true whether one considers basic research studies or more recent policy-oriented ones. However, the research has served to focus and clarify several important issues, thus indicating the cumulative impact over time of social science research on the perceptions and definitions of social problems (Bloom, 1966; Cohen and Garet, 1975; Cook and Lange, 1975; Getzels, 1969). These issues relate to the re-definition of school effectiveness in terms of output rather than in terms of input as well as to re-appraisals of methods of measurement and of methods of determining the relationships between measures in the educational context. What is needed now is further research relating to these issues.

The selection of dependent or criterion measures has also created problems in the interpretation of studies of school effectiveness and thus also merits further study. As we have seen, the most common criterion measures employed have been norm-referenced standardized tests of ability and attainment. Furthermore, only a limited range of measures of attainment has been used, tests which measure attainment in the basic curricular areas of English and mathematics. Tests of such subjects as physics or chemistry have been rare enough. A number of considerations lead us to suspect that this dependence on a limited range of standardized tests might tend to obscure the effects of particular school practices. It seems unlikely that tests designed to evaluate general individual student attainment would be sensitive to the objectives and content of school curricula in specific areas of attainment.

Given the fact that serious problems in the measurement of school effectiveness are still unresolved, general statements about the effectiveness or non-effectiveness of schooling in general or of school practices in particular are hardly justified. If research in the social sciences is to continue to make a contribution to the resolution of problems in education — albeit indirect and piecemeal — it is incumbent on social scientists to examine such problems systematically and empirically. Before this has been accomplished, it ill behoves the researcher to offer definitive advice on schooling to the policy maker or to the general public.

Chapter Two

The Present Investigation

A major problem in interpreting studies of school effectiveness relates to the appropriateness of the criteria used to measure school output. Most studies which have examined the differential effects of school have used standardized norm-referenced tests which had been designed to measure individual ability and attainment of a general kind (verbal and/or numerical) though there are several reasons for believing that such tests may not be sensitive measures of school or programme differences. In the present study, we use alternative measures of school output, which we believe are closely geared to the actual curricular activities of schools. These measures are the results of public examinations within the English educational system.

Public examinations

Public examinations play a very important role in 'European education. They serve three main functions: they act as summative measures of individual student attainment at the end of a course of study, they monitor the performance of schools, and they serve as instruments of selection for further education as well as for immediate employment in some cases (Nuttall, 1975). The advantages and disadvantages of public examinations have been a matter of discussion and debate for at least a hundred years (Morris, 1961; Nuttall, 1975; Wiseman, 1961). Among the main advantages that have been cited is the motivating influence of the examinations on students and teachers; among the disadvantages, the restrictive influence of the examination on the work of the classroom, both in terms of content covered and methods of learning, has been stressed.

The attribution of such strong effects to public examinations reflects the seriousness with which the examinations are viewed by European educationalists. Given the functions which the examinations are used to serve, this is hardly surprising. Besides, the existence of a system of public examinations inevitably results in a strong central control of the curriculum in the schools, much of which is mediated through the examinations themselves. Not only are examinations designed to reflect prescribed curricula which are followed in schools, but the curricula, in practice, are bound to reflect the examinations. Indeed, if there is a conflict between objectives which are explicit in the syllabus and objectives which are implicit in the examination, students and teachers generally choose the latter (Madaus and Macnamara, 1970).

Two systems of public examination exist in England: the General Certificate of Education and the Certificate of Secondary Education. The former has a strong academic bias and operates at two levels: one for pupils aged 14 years of age or more, and one for pupils aged 16 years of age or more. The Certificate of Secondary Education, on the other hand, is based on curricula that are more general and practical and is normally taken by pupils who are 14 years of age or more. Insofar as comparisons can be made between the two examination systems, a grade one pass on the Certificate of Secondary Education is said to be equivalent to a pass mark in a similar subject area on the General Certificate of Education at Ordinary level.

The General Certificate of Education (GCE) examination, which is the examination which concerns us in this study, was conceived as part of the general post-war period of reconstruction in England. In 1947, the authorities, conceding that some form of external examination was still essential for both entrance to university and professional bodies, proposed the GCE system. This, contrary to practice in previous examinations, consisted of a subject examination with no subject group requirement; if a candidate wished to offer only one subject, he had no obligation to offer more. Thus it was imagined that candidates would gain greater freedom in their choice of subjects. The examination was also conceived with the simple pass-fail concept. Those who passed would be given a certificate, those who failed would not.

In the post-1944 educational system in Britain, selection was applied not only to the school but also within the examination system. For the GCE examination, limitations were applied in the form of a lower age limit of 16. This meant that the Secondary Modern schools, established to run courses only up to the school leaving age of 15, were effectively excluded. To discourage use still further, the pass standard of the new examination was set at a higher level than its forerunners and, at first, schools were actively encouraged to enter only those candidates with a good chance of passing. This examination was designated GCE Ordinary (O) level and defined as representing an examination taken at the end of a five-year course in a secondary school. To accommodate university entrance requirements and provide an opportunity for specialization, a second level of GCE, Advanced (A) level, was established as an examination to be taken after a further two years study. Advanced level examinations have one unusual feature: there is no need to take a subject at Ordinary (O) level before attempting it at Advanced (A) level. Thus, a candidate who is likely to take a subject at A-level may by-pass the O-level examination in the subject. In practice, however, few schools use this option.

GCE examinations are conducted by eight independent examining boards.* Only two boards, the Welsh Joint Education Committee and Joint Matriculation Board, serve limited areas; otherwise, candidates may take examinations of any board. For example, candidates taking examinations of the University of London Board are drawn from all over England. All boards conduct summer examinations at both O and A-level and autumn examinations at O-level. Only two boards (Associated Examining Board and University of London) hold autumn A-level examinations.

The first GCE examination, held in the summer of 1951, showed that traditions of previous examinations prevailed. The apparent freedom of choice offered by the new system was restricted by the fact that schools offered a hard core of traditional subjects (for example, English Language, French and Mathematics). The limits constraining candidates to 11 O-level and four A-level subjects were rarely extended. Statistics from the last 15 years show that, on average, candidates take four O-level or two A-level subjects.

The limitations put into the regulations in practice proved useless.

---

* Associated Examining Board, Joint Matriculation Board, Oxford and Cambridge School Examination Board, Oxford Delegacy of Local Examinations, South University Joint Board for School Examinations, University of Cambridge Local Examinations Syndicate, University Entrance and School Examinations Council of the University of London, and Welsh Joint Education Committee. All except the Joint Matriculation Board, the South University Board and the Welsh Joint Committee have arrangements for students living overseas.

Schools opposed the age limit by claiming that many of their bright pupils were ready to take the examination at 15 years of age or less and, in 1953, this regulation was altered. The pass-fail concept has also been modified. In 1963, five official grades of pass were recognized at A-level. Provision was also made for candidates just failing to receive an O-level pass in the subject. In June 1975, O-level grades were officially recognized. (However, as this report deals with 1974 data, only the unofficial O-level grades used by the University of London were available.)

Outline of the procedure in the present investigation

The main purpose of the present investigation was to examine the relationship between student and school characteristics, on the one hand, and student achievement, on the other. The availability in England of a system of evaluation in which a wide range of the curricular activities of schools are examined separately, and in which examination performance may have serious consequences for the student, suggested to us that differences between schools in achievement so measured might be more readily explicable by differences in their resources than had been the case in research studies which had used standardized tests of verbal or numerical ability as their measure of school output. Furthermore, the examinations which interested us in England are taken at a level of education at which survival would have considerably reduced the differentiating effects of familial background on educational achievement. Thus, to some extent, family background factors are controlled and the opportunity for school effects to be demonstrated is further enhanced.

To carry out our investigation it was necessary to obtain data on students and on their environments, both within the school and outside it, as well as information on their examination performance. The examinations that were chosen for the investigation were the General Certificate of Education (GCE) of the University Entrance and School Examinations Council of the University of London (sometimes referred to as the London Board). Marks on examinations obtained by students in our sample, matched to their examination number, were supplied to us on magnetic tape by the London Board. Examination results were obtained for 11 subjects at the Ordinary level; Biology, Chemistry, Mathematics (Syllabus B), Physics, English Language, English Literature (Syllabus A), French, German, History (Syllabus B), Geography and Spoken English. Results were also obtained for four Advanced level subjects: English Literature, French, Geography and Pure Mathematics.

The design of our study anticipated four major classes of independent variables that might be employed in the explanatory model. Three of the classes were coincident with the information sources: those relating to schools, to teachers and to students. It was evident that any explanatory model must also take into account family data even though these data were gathered from the students. It was also evident that the data must be gathered in such a form that they could ultimately be allocated to sets, which in themselves were capable of being expressed as interactions between sources as well as in terms of the independent effects of these sources.

Dissatisfaction with the explanatory model employed in previous studies (*e.g.*, Coleman *et al.*, 1966) affected the nature of the data gathered. This dissatisfaction can be summarized in the form of a statement that the allocation of school achievement effects to the family, when family is represented by socioeconomic status variables, supposes that the intention of the school is to reduce between-social-class differences, when the intention of most schools would be seen to be to give to each child the degree of concern which is appropriate to his individuality. This involves advancing those who are better prepared for school instruction with as much effort and deployment of resources as is devoted to those who are less ready to take instruction. This led to an attempt in the present study to assess the effect of schools after the initial readiness of individual students for instruction had been partialled out. Many of the students in the sample would have taken a secondary school entrance examination administered by the Local Education Authority, and in most cases, although the entrance measures would differ for each authority, the standardization employed would have been scaled on national norms. Measures at entrance, however, would not be available for the Independent schools in our sample, nor would they be available in every case for Maintained and Direct Grant schools. Nevertheless, if entrance measures could be obtained, some attempt might be made to employ a different explanatory model.

To obtain information on the independent variables for our study, a sample of schools was drawn from Local Education Authority districts within which the majority of the London Examination Board Centres were located. Six districts were identified as meeting this criterion and were approached to obtain their cooperation. Two declined to cooperate. All schools with examination centres within the boundaries of the four participating authorities were approached, so long as the number of candidates entered in the previous year for the examinations exceeded ten. Of 64 centres approached, 48 agreed to cooperate; of these, 44 actually cooperated to the extent of returning questionnaires completed by principals, teachers and students.

In May 1974, the questionnaires had been sent from the School of Education, Bristol University to school principals, who were requested to organize their administration. One questionnaire was to be completed by the school principal (though if appropriate, parts could be completed by other members of staff), another was for completion by all teachers preparing students for the London Board examinations (Ordinary or Advanced level) in 1974, while a third questionnaire was to be completed by all students taking one or more Ordinary or Advanced level examinations in 1974. The examination numbers of students were entered on the student questionnaire for later matching with examination results. The final source of data for the independent variables was the so-called Form 7 (Schools), which contains information on school characteristics and is returned by schools annually to the Department of Education and Science. Information from this form was obtained from the Local Education Authorities. On completion, all the other questionnaires were mailed by schools to the Research Unit of the School of Education at Bristol University, before students had taken their examinations.

Analysis of data involved relating the information obtained in questionnaires concerning school, teacher and pupil characteristics to the performance of students on public examinations. Analyses were carried out separately for each subject examination taken at Ordinary and Advanced level (15 in all). One non-cognitive measure – that of a student's attitude to school – was also included as a dependent variable; this was because of the frequent accusation that studies of school effectiveness have placed too great a reliance on cognitive performance, to the neglect of other kinds of behaviour, as a measure of school outcome.

In our analyses, the amount of between-school variance in achievement in each dependent variable is compared with the amount of variance occurring within schools. The ability of our independent variables to predict each portion of variance (within and between schools) is then examined in regression analyses. Before final regressions were carried out, variables were assigned to a number of 'blocks' on the basis of their conceptual similarity and their empirical relationships with the criterion variables. Five blocks of variables, representing School, Teacher, Family, Individual and School-Individual, were created. Each of the blocks was considered to be capable of a unique contribution to explained variance in the achievement measures. In the final regression analyses, following the symmetric variance decomposition procedure used by Mayeske *et al.*, (1972) in their re-analyses of the Coleman data, variance explained in dependent variables is partitioned into a portion attributable to each block of independent variables uniquely and a portion attributable to all combinations of independent variables. This procedure has the advantage that the partitioning of variance is not dependent on the order in which variables are entered into the regression equations.

Chapter Three

Sample

Unlike studies which seek to make direct comparisons between populations as, for example, the studies of the International Association for the Evaluation of Educational Achievement (IEA) (Postlethwaite, 1975), or studies which seek to represent the population of a particular country, as the study of Coleman *et al.*, (1966), the present study was concerned with testing hypotheses about the effects of schools on achievement, and the sample was deliberately constructed to be homogeneous. It was more important to be able to include a variety of school characteristics within the sample than to ensure that the sample represented a given population. A further consideration, related to the first, was that the achievement data obtained should be as reliable as is ordinarily available and should encompass, not experimental performance, but performance which was accepted by schools as the measure of the success of their own curriculum. The priorities in determining the sample were therefore the existence of an examination system, accepted by a wide range of schools and representing a level of academic achievement which is publicly acknowledged both by universities and by employees, at a level of schooling where selective effects of the school system had already taken effect. Since public examinations were in question, it was most important that the examining board considered would be willing to cooperate to the fullest extent in making data available prior to the conduct of the examination and subsequently release marks rather than grades as measures of achievement.

The London University Schools' Examinations Board was chosen because it represented all of these qualities. It is an established examination board with a history dating from before the beginning of this century and is universally recognized by universities within the British tradition. While its catchment area for examinees extends through the length and breadth of the United Kingdom, the schools which employ the Board as their major examination medium are situated within a limited area surrounding London, mostly within the Home Counties. They thus represent a more homogeneous, geographically confined set of schools than would have been true of most other boards. In 1974, 191,000 candidates in 2,300 centres took the London Board examinations.

A further constraint upon sampling was that any approach to the schools (known by the Examinations Board as centres) required the prior approval of the Local Education Authority.* The majority of the schools came from the Maintained schools sytem; that is they are schools which are financed and administered as part of the state system of education by Local Education Authorities. However, the autonomy of the secondary schools is such that the principal or head teacher of a school would be free, despite the Local Authority's approval, to decline to take part in a scheme such as this. Apart from those schools in the fully Maintained system there are other schools whieh present pupils for London Board examinations. Such Direct Grant schools, which are outside the immediate control of the Education Authority, are usually administered through a Board of Governors and are more directly under the control of the head teacher. Independent schools also, as their name implies, operate outside the control of local or central educational authorities. They may however, invite inspection from the Department of Education and Science. Such was the case for all Independent schools which took part in the present study; furthermore, all had been 'recognized as efficient'. In general, Direct Grant and Independent schools have greater freedom to manage their own resources than have Maintained schools, which are more subject to official constraints. Since it was of the utmost importance that schools

---

*It was a misfortune of the study that it began in a year when regional reorganization was taking place and new Education Authorities were being formed out of older authorities with the consequence that the changing of boundaries disrupted the smooth recruitment of schools.

be recruited to the sample to represent the variety of school characteristics available, no attempt was made to carry through a prior stratification. Direct approaches were made to those Local Education Authorities within which the majority of the London Examination Board Centres were located.

Schools in London and the Home County Authorities are in general more likely to take the London Board Examinations for the majority of GCE candidates. Precise information on numbers taking examinations, however, was not available in advance and the only guidance we had before the registration of the candidates was the total number of candidates entered by a school in the previous year (1973). The first action in setting up the sample was to write to those Chief Education Officers of Local Education Authorities where the number of centres in that Authority and the number of candidates entered by each centre suggested that there would be a profitable return from the inclusion of schools from these Authorities. In some cases, letters were followed by visits, where the purpose of the project was outlined and, in almost all cases, careful consideration was given to the request.

The Education Officers in the Authorities were concerned over a number of points in the study. One of the first considerations was the extent to which an approach at this stage in the school year would be disruptive of the schools at their busiest time (spring and summer) and the extent to which the schools were already involved in curriculum renewal, supported by the Authority, or in research by some other agency, or in substantial organizational change, sometimes consequent upon the regional reorganization of Authorities. A second consideration was the nature of the information to be gathered. Teachers and parents in Britain are very sensitive to the supply of personal and family data and there is a general reluctance to sanction any study which would seek to gather such information. Teachers' organizations too are resistant to enquiries which in any sense might be interpreted as reflecting the opinion of one teacher upon others or that might be construed as such from the teacher's statement about the school. Related to this is the consideration of the anonymity of the respondents. While guarantees could be given that the Authorities and the schools would not be named, the degree to which data reported would make the schools and Authorities identifiable by readers gave some pause. For the purpose of the study it was necessary to be able to match the examination data derived from the candidate numbers supplied by the London Examination Board with the personal data supplied by candidates and by the teachers who were preparing those candidates for the examinations. Consequently, there were obvious ways in which the researchers could identify individuals.

School, teacher and pupil questionnaires had already been piloted before the approach to Local Authorities took place. This was necessary so that the Authority could decide whether or not it would wish to take part, given the data being requested. The reaction of Authorities was such that changes were necessary in the piloted questionnaires in order to make questions more compatible and to reduce the amount of time taken to complete them. Thus the size of questionnaires was substantially reduced, partly by making use of a less convenient, but nevertheless equally reliable, set of information available from centrally collected returns from schools to the Department of Education and Science. Permission to have access to these data was also a prerequisite of acceptance by the Authority.

In the last analysis, two Authorities declined to cooperate, leaving four Authorities agreeing to take part. All centres within the boundaries of participating Authorities were then approached, whether or not they were Maintained, Direct Grant or Independent schools, so long as the number of candidates entered in the previous year for O or A-level examinations was greater than ten. Centres which were not schools, *i.e.* technical colleges which were further education establishments beyond school leaving age, were not included. The four Education Authorities concerned can be described as follows: (i) a London borough, heavily urban in character and with a wide range of socioeconomic status of families resident there; (ii) a rural county containing few large towns and having the most dense population near the coast; (iii) a county bordering London with extensive suburban towns and cities but with a rural population extending to the coast; (iv) a county heavily used as a commuting area for London workers and with large towns rurally situated and with an extensive rural population.

Of the 64 centres approached, 44 cooperated to the extent of completing the whole procedure of returning school, teacher and pupil questionnaires. The reasons for questionnaires not being returned were various and included such factors as the ultimate withdrawal of the school before the questionnaires were completed, the fact that the school was not in that year entering any candidates for London examinations, postal failures which resulted in the loss of parcels, and delay in administering the questionnaires so that some pupils had left the school and were not returning before the examination results were

Table 3.1: Numbers of schools by type in sample compared with numbers in population of schools registered for the London Board GCE examinations.

Type of school	No. of schools in sample	Expected numbers
Secondary Grammar	9	8.8
Secondary Modern	11	8.8
Secondary Technical	0	1.3
Comprehensive Secondary	12	13.6
Other Secondary	5	2.2
Direct Grant	2	1.2
Independent	5	7.5
TOTAL	44	43.4

known. In some schools, student questionnaires were completed after students had taken their examinations; these were not included in analyses.

Table 3.1 gives the number of schools of each type in the sample as well as the expected number if the sample of schools were representative of those registered as centres for ULEB O and A-level examinations. A comparison of the actual and expected numbers of centres for each type of school demonstrates a reasonably good match. It is not uncommon for some confusion of classification to occur between Secondary Technical and Other Secondary schools and between Other Secondary and Comprehensive schools. Some Comprehensives are divided into Junior and Senior High Schools and are classified as 'Other Secondary'. Some former Technical schools have been combined with former Secondary Moderns and may be known as bi-lateral schools, which could be termed as 'Other Secondary' or 'Comprehensive'. A more critical comparison is between the selective schools (Grammar, Direct Grant and Independent) and the non-selective schools (Modern, Comprehensive, Technical, Other Secondary). Our sample of centres shows a slight bias towards 'non-selective' schools.

Table 3.2 presents a comparison of the numbers of actual candidates for O-level from each type of school with those expected for the London Board figures for 1972. Although there are some noteworthy

Table 3.2: Numbers of examination candidates in sample by school type compared with numbers expected* (O-level).

Type of School	No. of candidates in sample	Expected numbers
Secondary Grammar	774	848
Secondary Modern	447	291
Secondary Technical	–	53
Comprehensive Secondary	658	980
Other Secondary	378	159
Direct Grant	110	106
Independent	283	212
TOTAL	2,650	2,649

* The expected numbers were derived from the Annual Report of the University of London Entrance and Schools Examination Council for 1972–73. The centres were therefore those involved in the 1972 summer examinations.

differences, the relative numbers of selective and non-selective school candidates are exactly preserved in the sample. It is quite possible that differences between actual and expected numbers are the result of between-year variations in candidature for London O-level examinations. Each school may enter different candidates for different boards; thus the numbers of candidates coming forward from a school may change according to shift of preference for one syllabus or another.

Candidates differ in the number of subjects they take, so that another source of comparison is the number of subjects offered for O-level by candidates in each type of school. Table 3.3 compares the actual with the expected number of subjects offered. The table reveals a bias in the sample in favour of the selective schools when the number of subject entries is compared. This is mainly attributable to an under-representation of Comprehensive schools and an over-representation of Independent schools. A possible explanation of the difference, despite close correspondence of the sample and target population in terms of numbers of centres and candidates from different types of school, is revealed in an examination of the sex composition of the sample. The figures in Table 3.4 indicate that there is a very high over-representation of girls, which undoubtedly arises from the voluntary nature of the sample of schools.

Table 3.5 displays the distribution of sample schools by type, size

Table 3.3: Numbers of subjects taken by sample candidates by school type compared with expected numbers (O-level).

Type of school	Actual number of subject entries	Expected numbers
Secondary Grammar	5,242	5,619
Secondary Modern	1,096	936
Secondary Technical	—	133
Comprehensive Secondary	2,609	4,415
Other Secondary	1,628	669
Direct Grant	740	535
Independent	2,064	936
TOTAL	13,379	13,243

Table 3.4: Numbers of examination candidates in sample by sex compared with expected numbers (O-level).

	Numbers of candidates in sample	Expected numbers of candidates
Boys	861	1,333
Girls	1,789	1,317
TOTAL	2,650	2,650

and sex. It is clear from the table that the over-representation of girls was an inevitable outcome of bias in the sex of the volunteering schools. The most serious consequence of this is that, while amongst the non-selective schools there is virtually no bias, among the selective schools, boys are only able to secure representation from three smaller mixed and one smaller single-sex Grammar schools and one Independent school. The bias is starkly represented in Table 3.6 which displays the number of O-level candidates by sex in the selective schools.

Table 3.5: Sample schools by type and size of school and sex of students attending.

Type of School	Sex of Students	Boys		Girls		Mixed	
	Size of School	<800	>800	<800	>800	<800	>800
Grammar		1	0	4	2	2	0
Modern		0	1	2	0	4	4
Comprehensive		1	0	1	0	1	9
Other		2	0	2	0	0	1
Direct Grant		0	0	2	0	0	0
Independent		1	0	3	0	1	0

Table 3.6: Numbers of candidates in selective schools in sample by sex (O-level).

Type of school	Boys		Girls		Total	
Grammar	171	(22%)	603	(78%)	774	(100%)
Direct Grant	0		110	(100%)	110	(100%)
Independent	94	(33%)	189	(67%)	283	(100%)
TOTAL	265	(22%)	902	(78%)	1,167	(100%)

Since it is reasonable to expect that between-school variance in achievement will, to a considerable extent, be contributed to by the difference between selective and non-selective schools, the nature of the School and Teacher variables (insofar as these are confounded with sex of school) which enter the regression equations is likely to be influenced by the bias in sex of schools, as well as by the bias in sex of candidates.

While there is evident departure of the sample from each of the comparison populations, it is also evident that apart from the sex bias, the sample is not grossly atypical. Nevertheless, no claim is possible from the outcome of this study which could be generalized for the populations from which they are drawn. The outcome of the study must be interpreted within the context of the description of the sample employed, it being remembered that it is not possible to give comparative figures for each of the variables by which the sample is described in the study.

While the total sample comparisons are important to assess the fitness of the centres drawn to represent the population of centres served by the University of London Board, further data are required on the structure of each of the samples from these centres, associated with each of the 11 O-level subjects which formed the main bases for the regression analyses. Table 3.7 throws important light on the distribution of candidates and centres for each subject in selective and non-selective schools. The sex bias in the sample in favour of girls and the greater preponderance of candidates from selective schools is clear from the table. The latter is less a matter of the slight bias in the sample in favour of such schools than of the heavier academic involvement of selective schools. The self-selective process by which schools enter into candidacy for O-level examinations is also clear from the table; more boys are entered for some subjects and more girls for others. Only in the case of Physics is there a higher proportion of boys than of girls. Chemistry, Mathematics and Geography, in that order, have the highest proportionate representation of boys but in none of the other subjects does it exceed 27 per cent. In the case of Spoken English, it falls as low as 10 per cent. The implications become more complex when the proportion of boys and of girls who are in selective schools is considered. In five subjects (Chemistry, Mathematics, German, History and Spoken English), a higher proportion of boys than of girls came from selective schools. Yet clearly this is not correlated with the subjects in which there is a higher proportion of boys in the sample. The answer seems to be that in subjects which are more particularly associated with the opposite sex, only those whose chances are regarded as high are entered. This is evident in the case of Physics in relation to girls, where 75 per cent of girls are from selective schools and in the case of History for boys where 94 per cent of the candidates are from selective schools. English Language on the other hand, in keeping with its status as a basic subject requirement for all candidates, closely approaches to the proportion of the sexes in the sample as a whole.

Table 3.7 also displays the hazards to be faced in interpretation of the between-schools analysis. On an *a priori* basis, one would expect the achievement of candidates in selective schools to be higher than that of candidates from non-selective schools. Consequently, the between-school variance in achievement will be increased, the more nearly the numbers of selective and non-selective centres are to being equal. Also, the reliability of the means for centres will be a function of the number

Table 3.7: Numbers of centres (selective/non-selective) and of candidates (boys/girls) for each examination subject.

	No. of selective centres	No. of selective centres with ten or more candidates	No. and %age of candidates in selective centres	No. of non-selective centres	No. of non-selective centres with ten or more candidates	No. and %age of candidates in non selective centres	No. and %age of candidates who are boys	No. of centres from which they came	%age of boys from selective schools	No. and %age of candidates who are girls	No. of centres from which they came	%age of girls in selective centres
Biology	16	0	691 65%	18	10	370 35%	183 17%	14	63%	878 83%	31	65%
Chemistry	10	1	333 72%	11	9	128 28%	199 43%	13	81%	262 57%	13	66%
Maths. D	11	1	400 65%	13	5	218 35%	218 35%	12	73%	400 65%	21	60%
Physics	12	2	388 71%	16	9	162 29%	303 55%	16	68%	247 45%	18	74%
Eng. Lang.	15	1	937 49%	23	2	992 51%	445 23%	19	36%	1484 77%	34	63%
Eng. Lit. A	12	1	578 54%	16	5	486 46%	296 27%	14	56%	768 73%	23	59%
French	16	1	843 62%	16	5	508 38%	346 26%	15	53%	1005 74%	26	65%
German	15	4	299 61%	11	5	195 39%	126 26%	11	64%	368 74%	20	59%
History B	13	1	468 72%	5	1	180 28%	140 22%	5	94%	508 78%	16	66%
Geography	16	2	672 56%	20	2	536 44%	388 32%	19	42%	820 68%	30	62%
Sp. English	13	1	767 66%	9	0	398 34%	195 16%	6	79%	970 84%	21	63%

of candidates in these centres and, in general, the effect of unreliability will be a reduction of between-school variance. In six of the subject areas, there are more non-selective than selective centres and in four subjects the reverse is true, while in one, the numbers are equal. The numbers are grossly disproportionate in the case of History, where there are more than two and a half times as many selective as non-selective centres. Yet, in every subject, except English Language, there is a higher proportion of candidates from selective than from non-selective schools. In other words, the non-selective centres supply fewer candidates than the selective centres. This is emphasized by the number of centres which have less than ten candidates. It reaches its peak in the case of Chemistry where only two of the 11 centres have more than ten candidates, and is at its lowest in the case of English Language, where all but two of the centres have more than ten candidates. Thus, in general, the means for non-selective centres will be less reliable than those for selective centres. The most probable effect of this should be to reduce the between-school variance attributable to non-selective centres and to increase the between-school variance attributable to the differences between the block of non-selective and the block of selective schools.

It will be important in the interpretation of the regression analyses to keep in mind the differences between subjects in the structure of the samples. The effect of choosing O and A-level examination candidates ought to be to produce a decided restriction upon social class. Evidence collected for the Robbins Report and for OECD studies indicates that there is a disproportionately high reduction in the numbers of children from lower social classes who survive into the public examinations at this level. The inclusion in the sample of Direct Grant and Independent schools, where fees are payable and which are affected by the self-selective effects of parents choosing areas in which to live, in which opportunities exist for selective grammar school education in Maintained schools, ought to result in variation in socioeconomic status between schools being much larger than that within schools. Since no socioeconomic data are available for London Board candidates as a whole, the representativeness of the sample in these respects cannot be tested. Nevertheless, the social-class structure can be examined.

The education of parents for our study was categorized in terms of whether the parents had spent more, less or the same length of time at school as pupils completing O-level courses. Thus, parents with more than 11 years of full-time education were coded 1, those with 11 years

Table 3.8: Means and standard deviations of measures relating to social class of candidates.

	Father's education	Mother's education	Father's job
N	2,604	2,597	2,407
M	2.340	2.436	2.339
SD	0.845	0.763	0.857

were coded 2 and those with less than 11 years were coded 3. Father's occupation was coded on a scale 1—5, 5 being unskilled manual and 1 being professional-managerial. These variables were derived from the pupils' questionnaires. The head teachers' questionnaire also permitted an estimate of the social class composition of the school and was again coded on a scale 1—5, 1 representing entirely middle and upper class and 5, entirely working class. The means and standard deviations of scale values for father's and mother's education and for the class of father's job are presented in Table 3.8. The figures are for the total sample of O-level candidates in the study.

The distributions of both father's and mother's education are heavily negatively skewed as expected, indicating the preponderence of pupils whose parents had received less than 12 years of full-time education and the small number where it had been longer. The distribution of father's job indicated the expected restriction arising from the selective effects of social class upon educational survival. There is no indication of skewness, the average social class of father's job being clerical or executive, in contrast to the bias towards social class 4 that would have been expected in the population.

Between-school measures of social class yielded variance in all three variables which was much larger than that arising within schools (Table 3.9). Thus, the expected effect of social class upon entry into the Independent and Direct Grant schools is borne out and the between-school variance ought to make possible the demonstration of any unique contribution from family background to achievement variance that may be inherent in the sample. Sufficient variation to enable social background effects to be revealed would seem to exist

Table 3.9: Between and within-school variance in measures relating to social class of candidates.

	Father's education	Mother's education	Father's job
Between-School Variance	8.398	6.341	7.490
Within-School Variance	0.586	0.525	0.599
F	14.301	12.082	12.509
d.f.	43,2560	43,2553	43,2363

Table 3.10: Between and within-school variance associated with student age, number of O-level examinations taken and time spent studying.

	Age	O-level Total	Time studying
Between-school variance	49.797	277.999	32.878
Within-school variance	31.230	4.634	0.971
F	8.902	59.991	33.875
d.f.	43,2592	43,2596	43,2576

within schools when one remembers the scales from which they were derived. Nevertheless, when the numbers of candidates for a particular subject within each centre is small, the restriction could be severe.

The social class composition of schools, as derived from the principal teacher's estimate, yielded values not dissimilar to those derived from the pupils' questionnaire. The differences between the two scales must be borne in mind. The mean value on the principals' scale was 2.7 and the standard deviation 1.08. The selective association between social class and type of school is confirmed by the simple correlation relating SES to school type. In the case of Modern schools, it is .42, for Grammar schools, −.16, and for Comprehensive schools, .37. (The values for Independent schools were not obtained, because this school type was omitted in order to avoid effects of mutual exclusion in the intercorrelations for the main regression analyses.)

Finally, we will look at univariate data for the total sample for three further variables — age of student, the total number of O-level examinations taken by a student, and the number of hours per week spent studying by the student. The mean age of students in the sample was 196.78 months (SD: 5.62); the mean number of O-level examinations taken, 5.83 (SD: 3.01) and the mean amount of time spent studying each week, 5.12 hours (SD: 1.59). Here again, for each variable, we see differences in within- and between-school variance; greater variance exists between schools than within schools in all cases (Table 3.10).

We have provided no specific data for the Advanced level sample. Neither have we attempted to examine its representativeness. The reason is that, although numbers permitted four subjects to be analyzed, the sample was in general too small to draw satisfactory conclusions about its representativeness.

Chapter Four

Independent Variables

The independent variables were derived from four sources: a questionnaire to principal teachers, a questionnaire to teachers, a questionnaire to students and an official form returned by schools to the Department of Education and Science. The development of questionnaires was guided by the need to obtain data which would have three basic points of reference: characteristics of the school, characteristics of teachers in the school, and characteristics of students (including their home background). Obviously an attempt was made to select variables which were likely to be functional in the explanation of school achievements. The names of variables derived from the questionnaires, as used in the computer programme, are given in parentheses in the text which follows.

School questionnaire

This is the questionnaire completed by principals and concerned with variables that, in the main, are situational (*e.g.*, school location, and type of control) and institutional (*e.g.*, the structure of the school administratively, academically and domestically, and staff-student ratio).

School category. On a purely administrative basis, schools may be classified into Maintained, Direct Grant or Independent. If a school is fully maintained, then it will be administered by a specific Local Education Authority and it will have much in common with other schools in the same Authority in terms of the resources allocated to it.

Nevertheless, there could be profound differences in types of school within the same Authority. Thus, an Authority may maintain schools in the Grammar School tradition, which have a strong academic bias, as well as Technical and Comprehensive schools. The status of the school was known from the Department of Education and Science listing of schools and from Form 7 (Schools). Schools were coded as Direct Grant (DIRGRANT), Maintained (MAINTAIN) and Independent (INDEPENDENT).

Administrative structure of school. Head teachers were posed a complex set of questions, the purpose of which was to determine the degree of autonomy with which sub-units of the school conducted their affairs. The types of such organization of the school which are available to heads to manage are as follows:

(a) The school may be divided into 'houses' which are ordinarily composed of domestic units, intended to cater for the social aspects of caring for pupils. These houses are ordinarily given names and may or may not represent functional activities of the school throughout the year. In some Independent Schools, houses are teaching organizations as well as being domestic organizations. However, their teaching is ordinarily of an ancillary nature to the main teaching organized by the school as a whole. It caters for private study called preparatory work, or 'prep'; this is in some degree equivalent to the homework ordinarily set by the day schools for pupils to carry out at home.

(b) The school may be internally organized by year groups. In these cases, the year groups are made up of all children whose admission fell in a given year and they are subdivided into forms or class groups which are ordinarily taught together. The head of a year group would coordinate the activities of form masters or 'tutors', as they may be called, whose responsibility is the overall care of children in both their social and academic life.

(c) Schools may be divided according to groups of years. It is common to find a junior, a middle and an upper school. In each of these schools there may be a headmaster, subordinate to the overall school headmaster, but nevertheless functioning as an independent administrator in the particular unit for which he is responsible. In this arrangement, the subschool may be regarded as a school of a smaller size, since the resources available are ordinarily disposed in advance and pupils in the year-groups with which we are concerned would be contending for resources with others in the upper school.

(d) A further possibility is for the sixth form studies to be organized independently from the rest of the school. Sixth form studies may be so separated from the rest of the school that the pupils have their own spaces and are treated in a more adult manner than would be common in schools that did not so recognize sixth form status.

The purpose of questions relating to the administrative structure of the school was to determine to what degree autonomy of sub-units of the school was provided for, both in a sense of domestic organization and academic organization. As such, these indicators could be regarded as a means of qualifying school size. Most schools have some kind of year-by-year division; however, they may differ in other forms of organization. One part of a question relates to whether a division by houses exists (HOUSES) and another part to whether a stratification by years exists on a coarser grid than single years (YEARS). It seems clear that these divisions refer to a purely administrative decision; a qualification of these divisions in terms of the domestic and pastoral life of the school was called for in further questions. Thus information was obtained on the domestic autonomy (DOMAUT) and academic autonomy of units (ACAD). The questionnaire also asked principals to indicate which subdivision previously described would be recognized by the pupils. Completion of this question clearly indicated that heads expected pupils to recognize more divisions than they originally reported earlier in the questionnaire. This seems to reinforce the view that the earlier questions on divisions in the school were interpreted as referring to divisions for administrative purposes, while the question on divisions recognized by students was interpreted as referring to divisions in terms of the school activities which may not have an administrative equivalent. We had no alternative but to code information on the pupils' perceptions of divisions (as reported by principals) as a separate entry (PHOUSES, PYEARS).

Streaming practices. Schools were asked to indicate the extent to which they divided pupils into groups for teaching purposes in terms of the level of their achievement. The ethos of secondary schools has been conditioned to a large degree by a general condemnation of the practices of forming children into homogeneous ability groups. There have been a number of studies, the most substantial being that of Barker Lunn (1970), in which comparisons have been made between schools not only in terms of the physical organization of the children into homogeneous streams, but also in terms of the philosophy of teaching which guides the setting of the level of instruction for particular pupils by the school. As early as 1962, a comparison of 13-year olds' achievement in 12 countries had revealed that the highest standard deviation of measures on all tests was characteristic of England, Scotland and Wales (Foshay, 1962). This has been interpreted as being a function of practices which have grown up of streaming children from the age of seven onwards in Britain. In the present study, the philosophy of each of the schools was therefore examined in terms of the provision made for dividing children into homogeneous ability groups and, in the teacher questionnaire, specific questions were asked about the degree to which teachers directed their teaching toward individuals or towards the group as a whole.

Questions on streaming practice were asked with respect to each year of schooling and covered practices of 'setting' as well as those of streaming. The differences between these two practices is that, whereas streaming divides children into homogeneous ability groups for the whole of their instruction within the school, setting implies the division of students into homogeneous groups for particular subjects only. A related practice of 'broad-banding', implying coarser ability grouping in which there is less within-group homogeneity, was also identified.

In coding, it was acknowledged that there is a continuum of possibilities with complete streaming at one end and complete mixed-ability grouping at the other. Although any combination for each of the six school years is permitted, a distinct clustering of the responses was expected and in fact occurred. In view of the clustering perceived and the importance of the different years for the examinations, the following division was adopted. Years 1, 2 and 3 are considered to be the years remote from public examinations and are therefore grouped together. Years 4 and 5 are preparatory to O-level examinations. Year 6 relates to A-level examinations and is regarded as a third category. In the coding, therefore, Years 1, 2, 3 (STR1), Years 4, 5 (STR2), and finally Year 6 (STR3) were taken as three separate groups and within each of these groups a three-level coding was adopted to indicate entirely mixed ability, some streaming and finally, entirely streamed.

School provision. A measure of school provision, over and above the provision of mere classroom space, was obtained. Such a measure gives some indication of the financial provisions of the school but it can also be expected to be an index of the school policy in terms of the balance of emphasis between sports and academic pursuits, since the school capitation allowance can be used in different areas with some degree of flexibility by the headmaster. In view of the responses to this question and the very different areas covered by its parts, a grouping was adopted as follows. Laboratories for science subjects were grouped together (LABS); foreign language laboratory with sound equipment was grouped with projectors and television receivers as an indication of audio-visual aids (AVAS); and information on the availability of a guidance counsellor was treated separately (COUNS).

Number of CSE and GCE subjects offered by schools. The information obtained in reply to these questions was quite straightforward. The proportion of O-level GCE subjects to all subjects offered (O/EXAMS) was coded, as was the total number of O-level GCE and CSE subjects offered (EXAMS). Whether or not principals perceive examinations as restricting the school curriculum was also recorded (SUBREST).

Admission practices. Data on admission practice were sought in the interest of obtaining information on the kind and degree of selectivity employed by the school. Principals were asked to state whether LEA examinations had been the basis of recruitment of those children currently taking their O-levels and whether such practices still continued with new admissions. Characteristically, measures obtained by the Local Authority would involve a verbal and numerical reasoning test, known as an academic aptitude test, an achievement test in English and another in mathematics and would incorporate a primary head teacher's assessment. Innovations in selection before the introduction of comprehensive schools would still have been operative at the time at which the children in the study were selected and would have involved a rank order by the primary head teachers, scaled against the results of academic aptitude tests. The purpose of the scaling and quantification was to enable schools to be sorted in relation to one another by the adjustment of school means. Thus, within-school variation in the primary school would be represented by the rank order imposed by the head teacher and the between-school variation would be a function of the academic aptitude test. It was unfortunate that LEA and school records were generally not available and only in limited cases were the scores on the particular tests or the scaled head teachers' assessments available. The loss was such that only a limited analysis could be undertaken. Independent schools may employ the Independent Schools' entrance examination known as the Common Entrance Examination or set their own selection examination. This fact was also recorded. Some schools are specifically denominational and a question was directed at whether or not the denomination of the child was in any sense a criterion for admission. Some schools, particularly denominational and Independent schools, insist on interviews with the child and the parents before they will admit and this information was obtained through the questionnaire. Information on Denominational Preference (DENOMF) and Sex of the child (SEXPF) were taken to be special factors relating to pupil admission and were coded separately. All the remaining information on admission practices was entered in a factor analysis and the factor scores were used as indices in the final analysis (ADMISS1, ADMISS2) (*cf.* Table 4.1).

The factor analysis yielded five factors with eigenvalues greater than 1.0, which together accounted for some 64 per cent of the variance. Varimax rotation was performed but attempts to conceptualize the factors were disappointing. In retrospect there seemed to be good reasons for this. Components which one might expect to be present are degree of pastoral care in familiarizing the pupil with transition to the secondary school, degree of selectivity on the basis of academic criteria and degree of regard for parental preference. Although these components are present in the factors, they are confounded by a number of different ways of exercising pastoral care. Thus, for instance, if we look at the rotated factor matrix, it will be clear that the first three items: staff visit junior schools, children visit new school, parents visit new school are all expressions of pastoral care. Reference to the factor loadings, however, indicates that these three items are virtually orthogonal, and it becomes easier to see how this arises when we consider that for some schools visits to feeder schools would be impracticable while for others, visits by parents of prospective entrants might be regarded as inviting improper influence on the admission procedure. For still other schools, however, more than one such activity might be considered necessary for a proper degree of pastoral care to be exercised. Such conflict will diminish correlation between items which conceptually belong to the same category. Similar considerations may well apply to the items concerning zoning by Local Authority dictum or geographical catchment area. Rotated factors were as follows:

C

Table 4.1: Rotated factor matrix for admission data.

Response (abbreviated)	FACTORS					Commonality
	1	2	3	4	5	
Staff visit junior schools	-69	04	-03	17	42	68
Children visit new school	-07	-13	16	-04	81	70
Parents visit new school	04	-08	59	-33	18	49
Prospectus is provided	-12	02	-04	-71	-09	52
School has specific feeders	-63	37	09	-12	-03	56
There is geographically defined catchment	-01	12	01	-64	42	59
LEA have zoned catchment	-20	27	-26	-05	55	48
Guided parental choice	-20	17	76	15	-03	67
Marks are used as criterion	59	37	08	55	08	79
Exam by LEA or school	86	16	03	25	05	83
Applicant is interviewed	22	-82	04	-12	-14	76
Parent is interviewed	-13	-79	14	14	13	70
Report of last school used	70	-36	07	17	-18	69
Distance from home is considered	17	-17	61	20	00	47
Parent is old pupil helps	61	-05	39	-18	-24	62
Sibling is at the school helps	26	-40	59	-09	-15	61
Variance accounted for (%)	24	14	10	8	8	

Factor 1: Admission mainly on academic criteria (use of entrance examination and report from primary school; staff tend not to visit junior schools, school does not have specific feeders).

Factor 2: Emphasis on interview rather than examination results (emphasis on person-to-person contact: interview with applicant and applicant's parent).

Factor 3: Emphasis on family preference, with distance from home a criterion (emphasis on guided parental choice; distance from home relevant).

Factor 4: Prospectus provided, but no geographically defined catchment area; marks tend not to be used.

Factor 5: Pastoral care of child (children visit new school; staff visits junior schools; defined geographical catchment area).

Consultation of parents on academic matters. Principals were asked (yes/no) if parents should be consulted on academic matters (CONSULT).

Socioeconomic status of catchment area. Principals were asked to respond about the socioeconomic status of the student body in the school in terms of five categories ranging from 'all or nearly all the pupils come from upper or middle-class homes' to 'all or nearly all the pupils come from working-class homes' (SES).

Other sources of school information

A number of other details about schools was added to the school data file from other sources, mainly from Form 7 (Schools), which is returned by schools annually to the Department of Education and Science.

Location of school. In some ways, this is a misnomer because the intention is ordinarily to discover the degree to which the admission of the pupils to the school characterizes them as belonging to a particular type of community. The area in which the school is situated may or may not be definitive of the areas in which the pupils live and the urban-rural classification which is so often applied may miss the critical difference between pupils drawn from the centre of an urban to a suburban location, as contrasted with children who are brought from over a wide rural area to a school in the centre of a busy, urban complex. Such differences have become even more marked as the size of secondary schools has increased and as comprehensivization of the intake to schools has become more marked. It is also necessary to distinguish the catchment of the school in terms of its day or boarding facility, since boarding schools will ordinarily draw from a country-wide area and the characteristic of the schools' location may have nothing whatsoever to do with the nature of the school as an institution. The school's geographical location was identified by reference to a large-scale map of the area in which the school was situated. Schools were characterized as urban or rural merely to provide a base upon which subsequent qualification could be erected (POPUL). In the questionnaire, schools reported on their boarding or day practices and also on their admission procedures. That part of the questionnaire concerned with admission procedures identified schools which were allocated specific catchment areas, in which they would draw their children from the primary schools within that area or from a fixed set of primary schools, without territorial definition. Independent and Direct Grant schools, some of which may be boarding schools, would generally draw their children from a non-fixed catchment area, but would differ in the degree to which the pupils came from a nation-wide catchment or from a locally based intake. Subsequent factor analysis of the section on admission procedures identified the factor which indicated distance over which schools draw their intake.

Size of school. While school size may seem to be a fairly simple aspect of schools to represent and to be given by the total number of students in the school, certain complexities arise when size is to be incorporated into an explanatory model. Size is not independent of the internal organization of the school and is related to the number of children who are following studies beyond the compulsory age of attendance (16). While size might also be interpreted in terms of the number of teachers or in terms of the usable covered and uncovered area that the school occupies, it is apparent that numbers of children are in the last resort the safest guide to what is meant by this section. School size is interpreted to mean the number of pupils contending for instruction and pastoral care, and the staff space and facilities available in the school are then the measure of the resources for which these pupils contend. It is apparent that in the organization of any school, the headmaster and staff of the school must decide where their priorities lie and may dispose these priorities through suborganizations which are to a degree autonomous and may be regarded as schools within schools. It seemed important to distinguish the various distributions of resource insofar as they affected the children within the age group under study, by identifying the organizational patterns whereby such children were separately provided for. Thus two measures of size of school were obtained, one being the absolute number of pupils in the school as reported in Form 7 (Schools) on 1 January 1974 which is the first day of the second term (SIZE). (This represents a reasonably safe estimate of those who will complete the year, which runs from September to mid-July in most schools in the United Kingdom.) The second was the number of children aged 16 or older in the school on 31 August 1973 (PUPIL 16). In the case of fully developed schools, this figure provides an indication of the corporate academic aspirations of the school, since students at this age will usually be preparing for higher education.

Sex of students attending school. Inspection of Form 7 (Schools) to determine the predominant sex of students in each school revealed that each school was either entirely single-sex or its sex-ratio lay between the limits of 47 and 52 per cent. Consequently, three categories were coded: male (SSEXM), female (SSEXF) and mixed (SMIXED).

Pupil-teacher ratio measures were obtained in two ways. The first is the pupil-teacher ratio for the school as a whole (PTRATIO), while the second is the pupil-teacher ratio in classes where the pupils are mainly 14 or 15 years of age on 31 August 1973 (PTRAT14). This information is derived from Part C of Form 7 (Schools).

Proportion of male teachers in a school was also recorded (MTEACH).

Local Education Authority. The Local Authority in which schools were situated was entered into the regression analyses as a dummy variable; each of the four was coded dichotomously and the first three were entered into the programme.

School type. The relics of the tripartite system in England and Wales, following the 1944 Education Act, whereby secondary schools were divided into Modern, Technical and Grammar, remain. The Grammar schools were highly selective academic schools providing for those pupils who would enter the professions and the universities. The Technical schools were those intended to provide for pupils who demonstrated some technical bias. In practice they drew from those pupils who failed to gain admission to the Grammar schools and much of their work was imitative of the Grammar schools. The Secondary Modern schools were largely for those children whose particular proclivities were not identifiable at the point of admission at age 11 and who might at some stage demonstrate that bias and be transferred to Grammar or Technical school. Transfers were infrequent and it was common for Secondary Modern schools to develop academic, technical or pre-vocational streams themselves so that they did not need to move pupils to a different type of school. In general, the Grammar schools selected the top ten to 20 per cent of the pupils in the Authority in terms of assessed academic achievement at the age of 11 and the Technical schools, depending on the Authority, would then take the five per cent or so below that level and the Secondary Modern schools the remainder. The debate over comprehensivization led to a general adoption of a non-selective form of school which was larger than schools had previously been and which might reach the size of a six-class entry or greater, implying an intake of 200 pupils or more and an overall size of school of upwards of 1,000 pupils, in some cases reaching 2,500 pupils. This was in contrast to the Secondary Grammar, Modern and Technical schools which usually had a school size limit of about 750. Three school types were coded dichotomously: Secondary Modern (MODERN), Grammar (GRAMMAR) and Comprehensive (COMPREHEN). A category was also available for other types of secondary school (OTHERSEC).

Teachers' questionnaire

As we shall see more clearly when we come to consider the derivation of variables, the views and facts recorded in the teacher questionnaire occupy an interesting position in relation to the other two data files. Because teachers of a particular subject to London Board GCE candidates completed questionnaires anonymously, it was not possible in every case to identify from which of the teachers in a school, a student had received instruction in that subject. Moreover, a high proportion of teachers teach more than one subject to examination level. The contributions of each teacher to the teaching methods which characterize a particular subject must be represented for each of the subjects he takes. In order to handle this complexity in programme form, the teacher data file consisted not of individuals but of subject-individuals. That is to say, the responses of a teacher of three different subjects were recorded three times, once in conjunction with each of the subjects taken.

In analysing the data, examination subjects were taken singly, and only the responses of children taking that subject were considered. Likewise only those teachers of that subject were allowed to contribute to variables relating to teachers. Where there was more than one teacher of the relevant subject in a school, the school mean of those teachers was used.

However, it could be argued that teacher attitudes about schools reflect a corporate staff attitude of the school rather than a spirit which is subject-specific and which could therefore have a differential effect on subjects. For this reason two sets of teacher opinions, which will be referred to in due course, were not treated as subject-specific, but a school mean was formed across all teacher-subject entries and the outcome was treated as a school variable. It follows that, because of the way the teacher data were entered, such a mean is weighted in favour of the teachers of more than one subject. In considering this fact, it must be borne in mind that we have not sampled all teachers in a school and we have limited information on what teaching is undertaken by our sampled teachers in non-examination subjects and non-examination years in the school. It can therefore be argued that this mean of teacher-subjects is appropriate in estimating the climate of teacher opinion only in the examination years.

The teacher sample in schools is problematic in that it is one of the areas where it is difficult to be sure of the completeness of the sample. In sampling students, it does not matter greatly if some examination candidates are missed and, in sampling headmasters, it is easy to check that we have a school questionnaire returned for each school in which there are students. With teachers, however, we are dependent on a sample of teacher-subjects at examination level to enhance our knowledge of the school and yet we cannot check the returns at this level. In some subjects we have sampled students for whom there is no teacher response. Likewise we have teacher data, for which corresponding student data are incomplete. In these cases, correlations are calculated only on complete variable pairs.

Subjects taught. Teachers were asked to indicate all subjects they were teaching to students taking London Board Examinations in the year in question. Clearly some teachers were preparing examination students for more than one subject and, as already explained, in these cases the teacher is coded separately for each of the subjects he taught. In effect, therefore, the unit of information in the teacher questionnaire file is teacher-subject rather than the person. In our sample, there was a total of 25 different subject papers being taken for the London examinations but out of these we were able to identify only 11 subject titles which were both representative of the syllabus and contained a sufficient number of entries for results to be reliable. Each of these 11 titles was dealt with as a separate entity in analyses.

Training and experience. Experience was assessed in terms of time spent teaching GCE subjects. Years teaching experience was recorded in months (YREXP). Answers to a question which related to specialist training, when taken in conjunction with information on the subjects taught by a teacher, provided information on whether or not the teacher had had specialist training in the subjects he taught (TRAIN).

Adapting syllabus to meet group and individual differences. For O and A levels separately, teachers were asked firstly, if they adapted their teaching to take into consideration differences between groups (BTGP), and secondly, if they adapted teaching to take into consideration differences between individuals (BTIND).

Previous experience with present students. The eventual coding of this information answered the questions: has the teacher taught the same pupils for another subject previously (OTHERSUB) and has he taught the same pupils for the same subject previously (SAMESUB)?

Distribution of course work over time and revision. On the face of it, this seems to be a straightforward question about amount of course time and revision time, but the actual responses clearly indicated a misunderstanding, probably due to the fact that in the first response column, teachers were asked to reply by indicating the number of *terms*, and in the second response column, they were asked to indicate the number of *weeks*. The variables were coded WKTM and RVTM.

Methods, techniques and aids in teaching. Of all the questions on the teacher questionnaire, the one relating to methods, techniques and aids showed the largest self-evident difference between teachers teaching different subjects. To some extent this is to be expected, since certain types of teaching technique are traditionally associated with certain subject areas. As might be expected, an attempt to factor-analyse these data yielded factors which were largely associated with the original items of the question. This is not particularly helpful as an exercise in data reduction and as the raw categories were very clear, it was possible to use these with some exceptions: the exceptions referred to approaches or aids that were scantily used (*e.g.*, programmed texts, teaching machines). Fourteen variables relating to use of the following methods, techniques or aids were created: lecture method (LECTURE), discussion method (DISCUSS), writing periods (WRITE), dictated lesson notes (DICTATE), practical periods (PRACT), field trips (FIELD), project work (PROJ), tv transmissions (TV), films (FILM), radio (RADIO), tape recorder (TAPE), slide projector (SLIDE), film-strip projector (STRIP), and overhead projector (OHEAD).

Teachers' expectation of student work related to courses. Questions about teachers' expectations of the amount of time students should spend on home-work and private study worked reasonably well and responses were coded in a straightforward manner on a time dimension (HMWK, PRIV).

Use of past examination papers. Teachers were asked about their use of previous years' examination papers for setting actual timed exercises (PSTEVER) and as a guide to teaching the syllabus (PSTGUID). The item worked in a straightforward manner and was coded separately for O and A level subjects in terms of the categories provided in the question — often, sometimes, never.

Attitudes to examinations and learning. The degree of teachers' agreement with nine statements about examinations and learning was sought. An identical question appears on the pupil questionnaire. Responses to the teacher and pupil questionnaires were factor-analysed, and both analyses yielded interpretable, but slightly different, sets of factors which are discussed in the section on the pupil questionnaire. The factors derived from the factor analysis of teacher responses were used in assigning factor scores to both teachers and pupils (TOPIN 1, TOPIN 2, TOPIN 3, TOPIN 4).

Length of time teaching. Teachers were asked to indicate the number of years they had taught in their present school (YRSHERE) and the total number of years they had spent teaching (YRSTOT).

Teacher training. Information was sought on the type of institution in which teachers had received their training and the kind of qualification received. It was realized that this information ought to be assigned to some form of scale reflecting perhaps the total length of teacher training or its position on a scale which might be characterized on a scale from vocational to academic. The procedure, however, caused some unease because of the value judgments such a scale would imply. Eventually the following order was adopted and its general trend appears to have been vindicated by the correlations which resulted (QUAL). The order was: College of Education or Teacher Training College with Certificate; College of Education with Certificate and B.Ed; Technical College, Polytechnic or University with degree and diploma; Technical College, Polytechnic or University with degree and diploma and Post-Graduate Certificate or equivalent; some form of intermediate post-experience training; and finally some form of academic post-graduate degree such as M.Sc. or Ph.D.

Sex of teacher (TSEX).

Age of teacher was ascertained on a nine-point scale, on which age was categorized in five-year bands (20—24 years, 25—29 years, 30—34 years, etc.) (TAGE).

Pupil questionnaire

Although this questionnaire was completed by each pupil taking London Board examinations, a number of items were entered and checked by the school after the pupil had completed his section. The examination number was in most cases checked by a member of the school staff, who was also asked to enter data relating to characteristics of the pupil on his entry to the school. These data could take the form of a score on a verbal reasoning test taken prior to the child's transfer to secondary school and/or a scaled and quantified rank-order given by the head of the child's primary school. Such entry characteristics are usually held on the record card of each child in secondary school but are sometimes stored inaccessibly or discarded. Even in cases where these data were available to the school, it clearly would have involved an additional administrative burden to report them and we were only successful in obtaining entries for VR1 for about one-third of the student sample. So that the lack of this information should not impair the main sample in the analysis, this variable was only used in a series of supplementary analyses.

Age of pupil. The pupil was requested to give his age in years and months (AGE).

Sex of pupil (SEX).

Examinations being taken in the coming summer. The pupil was asked to list the examinations he would take in the coming summer. The information was not coded but was used for checking purposes. In particular, it was used during the data-cleaning stage to check examination results received on tape. The total number of examination subjects taken by the child was, however, recorded as a separate variable for each level (OLVLTOT, ALVLTOT).

Perception of school. In two separate questions, the student was presented with 19 statements representing facts ('school uniform must be worn') and opinions ('school is enjoyable') about school and was asked to indicate whether he regarded the statements as true, false or was not sure. The 19 responses from both questions were pooled and coded in terms of the response to the 'True' column. The data were then factor analyzed. Seven factors emerged with an eigenvalue greater than 1.0, which together accounted for 52 per cent of the variance. The first common factor accounted for 13 per cent of the variance. The seven factors were then rotated by the Varimax method. Identification of loadings with an absolute magnitude greater than 0.03 enabled us to characterize the factors in the following way in terms of pupil perceptions (*cf.* Table 4.2).

Factor 1: Traditional and conservative in behaviour and academic. (Teachers expect pupils to stand when they enter and are strict about homework and discipline. School uniform must be worn and one has to be bright to get to this school.)

Factor 2: Academic by reputation. (You do not stand a good chance of getting to university and do not need to be bright to get to this school. Job prospects are not good. Pupils may not sit in during break; there is not a good choice of subjects and school uniform need not be worn.)

Factor 3: Good habits plus self-expression. (Good behaviour is not more important than good marks and pupils do express opinions which differ from those of the teacher.)

Factor 4: Unstructured, rule-free. (Pupils may not enter on arrival at school, may not choose where they sit in class, and they may not sit in class during break.)

Factor 5: Intolerance of less academic pupils and alienation. (Teachers discriminate against lazy and less clever pupils and are only interested in bright pupils. Going home is like entering a different world and school is not enjoyable.)

Factor 6: Hard work and acceptance of given material. (Success does not depend on hard work and pupils often express opinions which differ from those of teachers.)

Factor 7: Sport and adaptability to student makes school enjoyable. (Sport is important, there is a good choice of subjects and school is enjoyable.)

Factor scores, based on these factors, were entered into the regression equation and they form the group of variables designated as SOPIN1 to SOPIN7.

Attitude to leaving school. The student was asked how he would feel if he had to leave school immediately. Response categories ranged on a six-point scale from 'very happy' to 'I would do almost anything to stay at school' (ATTITUDE).

Table 4.2: Rotated factor matrix for pupils' perceptions of school.

Questions (abbreviated)	Factors (x 100)							Commonality
	1	2	3	4	5	6	7	
Pupils rarely express opinions	03	20	−41	10	11	−48	−06	47
Pupils may not sit in during break	13	36	09	41	06	−22	25	44
Pupils can enter on arrival	16	13	−08	−71	00	00	16	59
Pupils choose own place in class	−04	−02	15	−71	00	−06	−07	53
Good behaviour more important than marks	00	−06	−85	03	−03	07	03	74
Teachers expect pupils to stand	71	−12	−06	−10	01	08	−13	55
Teachers strict about homework	71	04	12	−04	−02	−10	08	54
School is enjoyable	−10	−18	−14	−18	−43	−15	42	48
Teachers strict about discipline	69	−04	−16	05	11	−02	11	53
Teachers discriminate against lazy and dull	03	−12	01	03	68	−11	10	50
School uniform must be worn	53	−31	05	02	07	−02	−15	41
Success depends on hard work	02	−13	12	−06	−01	−81	01	68
Sport is very important	06	05	−04	02	13	14	78	66
Home is like a different world	13	−08	−03	−08	58	13	−06	39
Teachers only interested in bright pupils	−03	13	−02	02	64	−09	−01	43
This school ensures good job prospects	13	−49	−22	−05	09	−15	04	34
You have to be bright for admission	45	−53	21	08	09	03	−07	55
You have a good choice of subjects	−17	−33	08	00	−18	−16	52	47
You stand a good chance of university	12	−68	06	06	−08	05	14	51
Variance accounted for (%)	13	9	7	6	6	5	5	

Perception of own ability. The student was asked to compare on a five-point scale how bright he perceived himself in relation to other students in his year (STATUS).

Academic aspirations. The student was asked to indicate on a five-point scale, ranging from his present position to university education, how far he would like to go with his education (ASPIRE).

Parents' education. Information on parents' education (father and mother separately) was obtained in a relative form. The student was asked, if at O-level, he had a longer full-time education than his parents had had (FAEDU, MAEDU).

Job aspiration. The student was asked to state the name of the job he would like to have. The specified job was subsequently coded in terms of the Registrar General's definition of jobs into a five-point scale, corresponding to socioeconomic classes 1 to 5 (JOBASP). The student was also asked to state his father's job. This was also coded using the Registrar General's classification (FAJOB). Finally, the student was asked to compare the status of the job to which he aspired with the status of his father's job on a number of dimensions — less or more manual, skilled, money, lesiure, clerical, responsibility, professional (JOBCMP).

Perception of teachers' expectations. The student was asked to indicate how good he thought his teachers expected him to be at his school work (one of the best, above the middle, in the middle, good enough to get by, at the bottom). A distinction was drawn in the question between the students' best subject (TCHEXP1) and his worst subject (TCHEXP2).

Pace-setting in pupils' school work. The student was asked to rank from the most important to the least important a range of people (friends, teachers, parents) in terms of their role in acting as pace-setters for his work at school. Coding presented some problems since the response categories that were presented differ in kind from one another. Option 1 ('No one. It's up to me') is clearly related to the independence of the respondent. Options 2 and 3 (friends at school and friends outside school) might be expected to indicate some relationship between the student's aspirations and aspirations in his neighbourhood. Option 4 (teachers) relates to school pressure, while two further options (siblings, parents) relate to family pressure. Because of the diversity of sources of pressure in this question it was eventually coded in parts. Because option 1 stands alone it was coded in isolation and assigned to the Individual block and coded as IPACE. Options 2 and 3 were taken to be signs of peer-press and the mean rank ordinal for these was coded as FRSPACE in the Individual block. Options 5 and 6 were taken together as family pace (FAMPACE) and their mean rank ordinals taken. Option 4 (teachers) was discarded.

Time spent studying. The student was asked the amount of time, in hours, he spent studying each week (MSTUDY).

Help with home-work. The student was asked to indicate if anyone helped him with homework outside school and if so, who helped (parents, siblings, friends). The item was re-interpreted into two parts, indicating a distinction between family help and peer help. Responses to the options relating to father, mother and siblings were taken as indices of family help (HMHELP); responses to options relating to friends were taken as indicating peer-help (PRHELP).

Attitudes to examinations and learning. The items relating to attitudes to examinations and learning on the pupil questionnaire are identical with those in the teacher questionnaire. The responses of students were coded dichotomously in terms of the 'Agree' response. The analysis of student response yielded three common factors with eigenvalues greater than 1.0, accounting for 43 per cent of the variance. These were subjected to orthogonal rotation using the Varimax criterion and yielded the following characteristics in terms of loadings exceeding 0.3 (Table 4.3).

Factor 1: Concern with pupils as individuals. (This school is important even to poor achievers and it is equally concerned for all pupils. Its teaching enables pupils to be responsible for their own learning and taking examinations makes them work harder.)

Factor 2: Pressure to do well in examinations. (Candidates feel under pressure to do well in examinations. Teaching is exam-oriented and examinations limit the teaching. Preparation for later study is more important than examinations and this school is not equally concerned for all pupils.)

Factor 3: Study more important than examination performance. (Passes in O and A-level examinations are not useful to pupils after they leave school. Preparation for later study is more important than examinations and taking examinations does not make pupils work harder.)

By contrast the teacher responses yielded four factors with eigenvalues greater than 1.0, accounting for 58 per cent of the variance. These were again subjected to orthogonal rotation and gave rise to the

Table 4.3: Rotated factor matrix for pupil and teacher attitude to examinations and learning.

Questions (abbreviated)	PUPIL FACTORS			TEACHER FACTORS			
	1	2	3	1	2	3	4
Passes in 'O' and 'A' are useful	09	07	−66	15	14	43	38
Taking 'O' and 'A' stimulates hard work	34	20	−53	07	−13	75	08
Exams limit teaching	05	59	25	−07	82	−08	00
Teaching is exam oriented	−21	59	−16	15	72	08	−14
Prep. for later study has priority	17	36	56	−80	03	−21	05
This school teaches responsibility	50	−01	−07	−20	01	01	67
This school has equal concern for all	63	−30	−06	−04	−20	07	75
This school is important to poor achievers	71	10	00	−54	−22	26	29
Candidates feel under pressure	02	65	−10	−39	22	57	−41

following factors:

Factor 1: Study important to all. (Preparation for later study is not more important than examinations. This school is not equally concerned for all pupils and candidates do not feel under pressure to do well in examinations.)

Factor 2: Focus of study is on examinations. (Examinations limit what pupils are taught and teaching is exam-oriented.)

Factor 3: Examination performance is more important than study. (Examinations make pupils work harder and candidates feel under pressure to do well. Passes in examinations are useful to pupils after they leave school.)

Factor 4: Concern with pupils as individuals. (This school is equally concerned for all pupils and the teaching enables them to be responsible for their own learning. Candidates do not feel under pressure and passing examinations is useful to them after they leave school.)

In order that the pupil's opinions should be represented in terms of the dimensions perceived by the teachers' frame of reference, the factor score coefficients for the teachers were re-entered into the analysis and used to derive four pupil variables. The within-school portion of the analysis therefore depends in this case on the deviation of pupil opinion from that of the corpus of subject teachers.

Chapter Five

Dependent Variables

The dependent variables in the study are 11 Ordinary level and four Advanced level examinations of the General Certificate of Education examinations set by the University Entrance and School Examinations Council of the University of London. Subjects at the O-level were chosen as being representative of the whole school curriculum and as having an adequate sample size. At the A-level, numbers were smaller and were adequate only in the case of four subjects. Table 5.1 contains a list of examination subjects together with the numbers of candidates and schools for whom examination scores were available for the present study. In addition, students' attitude to school (ATTITUDE) as measured in the pupil questionnaire of the present study, was included as a dependent variable. The student's attitude was scored on a six-point scale; a positive score indicates he is very keen to stay at school; a negative score that he would like to leave school.

In this chapter we shall first of all outline the general procedures adopted by the Board in marking and grading GCE examinations. It should be noted that while official results are given in the form of a letter grade, we had available from the London Board the numerical score on which grades were based. Secondly, we shall provide examples of the types of question used in the GCE examinations. And thirdly, we shall consider the GCE examinations of June 1974 (on which our data are based), paying particular attention to measurement characteristics of the papers.

Table 5.1: Dependent variables together with numbers of candidates and schools for whom scores were available.

Subject	No. of students	No. of schools
Ordinary level		
Biology	1,060	35
Chemistry	461	21
Maths (Syllabus D)	618	24
Physics	550	28
English Language	1,929	37
English Literature (Syllabus A)	1,064	28
French	1,351	32
German	494	26
History (Syllabus B)	648	18
Geography	1,208	37
Spoken English	1,165	22
Attitude	2,642	44
Advanced level		
English Literature	374	20
French	201	20
Geography	211	20
Pure mathematics	193	21
Attitude	832	22

Marking and grading of GCE examinations

The University of London offers candidates a wide choice of subjects, 72 at Advanced and 100 at Ordinary level. Thus subject control might be deemed a formidable task. In practice this is not the case. Each subject or subject group is controlled by an advisory panel consisting of both subject specialists and practising teachers at both secondary and tertiary education levels. The practice of accepting teacher nominations from the teacher unions is one which has ensured the involvement of practising teachers in the examination scene. Advisory panels can best be described as a central forum for discussions, syllabus revision, question paper format and content.

Chief examiners are appointed by a selection committee composed of advisory panel members and at O-level are often practising teachers. For most subjects, two chief examiners are appointed. Besides setting the question papers they supervise a team of assistant examiners who mark the papers and they exercise an overall responsibility for the examination. A chairman or moderator, usually a person with past chief examiner experience, is also appointed for each advisory panel. He serves an important role not only in the forum of the advisory panel but also in the general administration of the examination and by his advice to the governing council of the examining board.

The detailed way in which the papers are set depends to a large extent on the examining technique used. In setting multiple choice papers for example, teams of writers prepare the individual items which are then reviewed and pre-tested. Chief examiners select the 50 or 60 items for the examination from the prepared bank of items. In some subjects, structural question papers are prepared in a similar way. Teams of writers prepare the individual questions from which the chief examiners make a selection, among which they may include items of their own. Draft papers are sent to the chief examiners and moderators for comment. It is the moderator's duty to scrutinize the papers and to see whether the questions cover and are relevant to the syllabus, are of similar standard to previous years and, most important of all, are solvable. Subsequent meetings arranged between chief examiners and moderators serve to provide a final revision of the question paper content. Papers are also looked at and worked by a completely independent scrutineer. The papers are then printed in the numbers required for the examination.

In most subjects, the entry is large enough to preclude the chief examiners marking all the scripts. Teams of assistant examiners, each marking about 500 scripts are employed; for example, in a subject like English Language, with 30,000 candidates, more than 100 examiners are used. Thus, consistency between examiners is of paramount importance. The detailed marking procedure (marking scheme) prepared by the chief examiners helps to ensure that the abilities rewarded are equivalent for all.

Clearly the type of scheme is very much subject dependent. In Mathematics it is comparatively easy to produce a detailed scheme to award a fixed number of marks for method, accuracy, results, etc. In English Literature it is more difficult. In some subjects, essay questions are marked purely by impression. However, this practice is waning. The introduction of different forms of assessment techniques, including a more structured type of essay question, has facilitated the use of detailed marking schemes and hence more objective marking.

A copy of the marking scheme is given to each examiner taking part in the marking and his script allocation of approximately 500 is sent directly from the centres concerned. The results from a sample of this magnitude serve to give a statistically representative picture of the examiners' marking behaviour. Before starting his marking proper, each assistant examiner is required to run through, and mark, a small sample of about 20 scripts from his allocation. A coordination meeting held at this stage serves as a forum for examiners to discuss candidates' work and to alter the marking scheme in the light of their preliminary findings. A second task of this meeting is to divide the examiners up into teams of not more than 15 examiners, under the direction of a chief examiner. It is common for chief examiners themselves to mark relatively few scripts. Their major task is the supervision of their team. A chief examiner is usually able to assess the success of a paper by marking about 150 scripts. Soon after coordination, examiners send a batch of about 50 scripts to their team leader who will check for, and feed back, any possible bias or misinterpretation of the marking scheme.

A full statistical picture of results is produced about a week after the end of the marking period. The chief examiners then meet for a 'standardization' meeting. This, the most crucial of the whole examination process, is the one that determines the grading and hence the pass/fail point of the whole examination.

It is perhaps pertinent at this stage to say something about the distribution of marks of an examination. The graph in Figure 5.1 compares directly the marks gained by the examiner's group with those gained by the rest of the candidates. The tolerance bands give some indication of the expected variation in standard.

However, it is not enough merely to investigate marking behaviour and to look at the overall pattern; chief examiners must look carefully at the quality exhibited by the group of centres allocated to each examiner. For each centre in the group, tables are given comparing the two previous years' pass percentages with entry figures and performance in the current examination. In each of the three years, the centres will have been marked by different examiners to avoid possible bias. Looking at these records will confirm or deny the chief examiner's impressions. An examiner appearing lenient on the basis of his overall statistics may prove to have a group of schools with high achievement

Figure 5.1: Examiner statistics, cumulative mark distribution for one examiner.

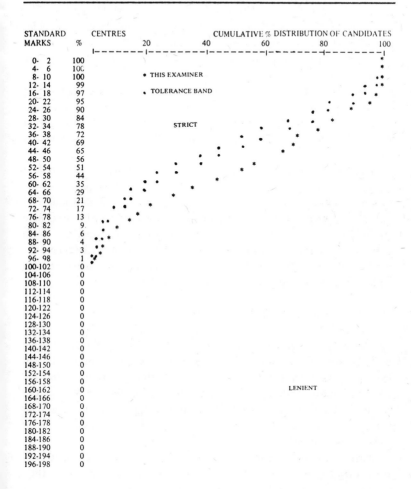

STANDARD MARKS | % | CENTRES | CUMULATIVE % DISTRIBUTION OF CANDIDATES

over the years. On the other hand, schools with consistent numbers of entries, but significant changes in performance in the current examination, will alert the chief examiners to possible severity or leniency.

Generally, the two sets of statistics, together with the chief examiner's impressions, are sufficient to make recommendations for examiner adjustment. Sometimes, however, it is necessary to scrutinize more scripts before a decision can be reached.

The tables of statistics for individual schools are generally more valuable at Ordinary level, where the numbers of candidates are large. At Advanced level, the small numbers of candidates entering, together with the variation in subject entry from year to year, make the statistics of little use.

Another possible way of checking examiner's standards is to look at the performance of that group of candidates on other papers in the examination. This is particularly valuable in subjects with a multiple-choice component like O-level Mathematics, Chemistry or Physics. Here the multiple-choice test, with its totally objective marking, acts as an external standard. By examining the mean relationships between the two sets of scores for each group (examiner), chief examiners are both able to discern and quantify variations in standard.

The example given in Figure 5.2, illustrates essay and multiple-choice paper scores for four examiners A, B, C, D. In each case, a good correlation between the two measures enables the data for each examiner to be represented as a straight line. The separation between the lines gives a measure of the variation between examiners. In this example, examiner D seems the outlier. Although his scores on the essay paper vary little compared with those of his fellows A, B and C, the high scores on the multiple-choice paper suggest that the examiner may be too severe. An adjustment of +10 marks is necessary to bring the examiner into line.

With all this evidence, chief examiners are in a position to make their recommendations for adjustment of individual examiners. It is their next duty to compare the statistics relating to any team of examiners and to make sure that all the teams are conforming to the same standard. Team statistics are based on 5,000 or more candidates and thus provide a statistically representative cross-section of the candidate population. One or two 'rogue' examiners in a team will not affect the picture to any large degree. Having ascertained this, the examiners are in a position to consider the subject as a whole.

Statistics are presented for each subject in terms of 'standard'

Figure 5.2: Examiner adjustment using multiple-choice paper scores

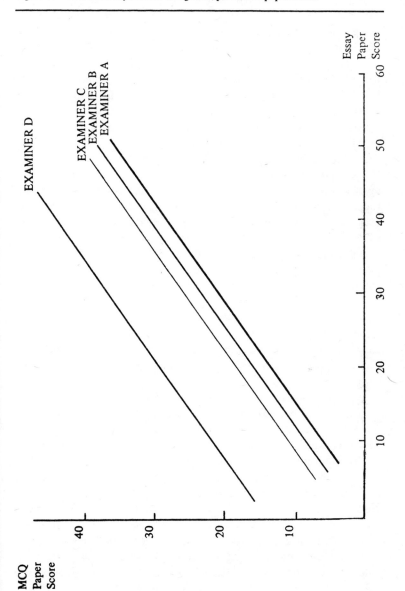

candidates. This group, consisting of the school population in a subject, can be considered relatively stable in ability from year to year. External candidates, together with those from further education centres besides being a small proportion of the entry, are considered more un-predictable in standard and are excluded. Cumulative mark distri-butions are given for each paper and the subject as a whole and, as for individual examiners, the distributions are given in graphical form. Data from the current examination is backed up by statistics from previous years. The very definition of the term 'standard' candidates implies a consistency in performance between successive years, providing the scheme of examination has remained unaltered.

Radical differences in distribution are more likely to be caused by the examination than by the ability of the candidates. This is not to say, however, that the group will remain constant over a long period in time. Subject popularities do change. The last decade has been characterized by a movement away from the science and classical subjects. In particular, the movement away from subjects like A-level Botany and Zoology to A-level Biology has resulted in a changing population. The introduction of different syllabuses and examinations will also affect the population. A new syllabus may start with an entry from a few good schools and consequently higher ability candidates. As more schools enter, standards will drift towards the norm. Thus in fixing their standards, chief examiners must be aware of any changes in entry patterns characterized by a sudden rise or fall in entry numbers. The analysis of data from successive years provides a good indication of such trends.

Chief examiners must also be aware of changes within the school system. The school leaving age was raised in 1974 from 15 to 16. It is too soon yet to assess the true effect of this. However, it is likely that the move will affect entries. The increase in subject entry for Art and English subjects may be evidence of this.

When all the adjustments have been considered and standards fixed relative to previous years, the marks must be converted into grades. The Advanced level examination has an official grading system which is common to all examining boards. The system, as prescribed by the Schools Council, defines five A-level pass grades denoted A, B, C, D, E in descending order of merit and two fail grades, O, equivalent to an O-level pass, and F to indicate complete failure. An approximate percentage for each grade is also suggested as given below.

A-level grade	Cumulative percentage
A	10
B	25
C	35
D	50
E	70
O	85—90
F	100

These percentages were not put forward as a hard and fast rule but more to serve as guidelines for A-level grading. In general most A-level subjects achieve a pass rate of between 60 and 70 per cent.

Different Ordinary level grades are awarded by the eight examining boards. The University of London awards five grades, three pass, A, C, E and two fail, F and H. No fixed proportions are specified for each grade. However, it is likely that between five and ten per cent are awarded a grade A and 50—60 per cent achieve a pass.

At both levels, examiners usually start in their grading task by fixing the pass/fail point. By this stage in the standardization procedure, they have a good idea of the standards and it usually involves little discussion to arrive at this important borderline. Often chief examiners may refer back to scripts to reinforce their opinions.

At A-level, the stipulated percentages serve as a guide for the other borderlines. At O-level, chief examiners rely more heavily on their experience as examiners. In deriving the actual mark values for both levels, the chief examiners use their experience of the examination itself and their intuitive criteria for the grade values.

The principle of grades with stipulated percentages, as in the A-level scheme, has much to commend it. Without it, comparison of standards between subjects and between boards, particularly for the purposes of university selection, would be a difficult and almost impossible task. To many candidates the award of a particular grade is crucial; it may mean the difference between being awarded a university place or not. Thus it is critical to minimize the risk of misclassification, particularly for the A-level pass grades.

Ironically, the most critical points B/C, C/D, D/E all come by virtue of their definition at the middle of the distribution where discrimination is least and where the difference between a grade B and a grade D may be as little as six marks. As far as possible, examiners try to avoid fixing grade boundaries at peaks in the distribution.

The chief examiner's role in an examination does not end when he determines a set of grade points. An extensive reviewing of borderline scripts is further assurance of any candidate's correct grading. In addition, chief examiners compile reports on success and failure in the examination, in which they try to point out the errors and omissions of candidates. The feedback of these reports to teachers is considered an integral and important part of the examination cycle. The reports not only influence teaching in schools but also act as one link in the communication of ideas between chief examiner, teacher, teacher-union and advisory panels.

Question types used in the GCE examinations

1. *Essay questions.* Even though different forms of examining are used extensively in O-level examinations, essay questions are still the primary testing mechanism at A-level. As might be expected, there are varying interpretations of the 'essay' theme; most however fall into the 'discursive', *i.e.*, 'describe and discuss' category. Two examples taken from A-level Biology are as follows:

> Describe the methods by which two named animals and two named plants survive adverse environmental conditions.

> 'Careful application of ecological principles is essential for the survival of man.' Expand and discuss this statement.

Well-thought-out essay questions and marking schemes can be used to discriminate effectively among candidates. Inconsistencies may arise when more open-ended questions are given as in, for example, the question:

> Argue the case for or against the study of the history of Biology.

Here, the nature of the question lends itself to a more subjective type of marking. In consequence, it may prove more difficult to maintain equivalence in standard over questions. Some questions may be 'easy options'.

Essay papers traditionally offer candidates a wide choice of question. In doing so, they limit syllabus coverage; the prescribed number of questions is often small, usually four or five. Other criticism may arise from the fact that this wide choice of questions leads to many different examination papers being set or to inequable benefit by reason of choice.

2. *Structured questions.* In the past few years, structured questions have been introduced into many O-level subjects including Chemistry, Biology, History and Geography. Nevertheless there is often confusion about the definition of the question format. In general terms, a structured question may be defined as a question on a particular theme or topic which consists of a distinct number of parts requiring fairly short answers. In most cases the answers are written directly onto the examination paper. Thus, structured questions have the advantage of an inherent, detailed mark scheme, making marking both easier and more objective. An example, as used in an O-level Chemistry examination, is given in Figure 5.3. There are various ways of structuring questions. The example cited is a question which has been structured by *difficulty*. The idea is that the early parts should contain enough material suitable for the weaker candidates, while the later parts should search the better candidates.

Sometimes this kind of difficulty structuring is not possible. In Chemistry and Biology, it is often the case that a certain logical order of sub-questions must be maintained at the expense of the difficulty structure. Experience has shown that there is no reason to suppose that this approach is any less valid.

Structured questions are commonly centred on stimulus material given as a piece of original evidence, *e.g.*, a newspaper report, scientific findings, electron micrograph, photograph, etc. This stimulus is used to trigger-off a pattern of recall and to induce a particular train of thought from the candidate. Thus, it aims to test most of the skills, *e.g.*, knowledge, comprehension, to some degree. An example, taken from O-level History, is given in Figure 5.4.

3. *Short answer questions.* A short answer question provides a vehicle for testing a combination of factual recall and an ability to produce a terse, compact answer. The following list illustrates the different forms of construction: short answer (single person or object); arrangement in chronological or some other order; completion of sentence or paragraph; write a sentence; tick a box or underline a word; match lists, mark or label on a graph, diagram or photograph; measure a graph; solve a small 'numeric' problem. Illustrative examples taken from Physics and History are given in Figures 5.5 and 5.6.

4. *Multiple choice questions.* In the 1960s, many O-level subjects

---

Figure 5.3: Structured question — O-level Chemistry

2
SECTION A
Answer TWO questions.

Relative atomic masses (atomic weights) and other data will be found on the front cover.

1.   The apparatus shown below was used to prepare a sample of anhydrous iron(III) chloride, $FeCl_3$

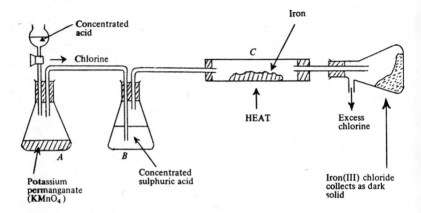

(a) Name the acid which is run into flask *A*.   (2 marks)

(b) What is the purpose of the concentrated sulphuric acid in flask *B*?
                                                                         (2 marks)

(c) Write an equation for the reaction taking place in tube *C* between iron and chlorine.   (2 marks)

(d) 0.5 mole of chlorine molecules, Cl_2 is passed over excess iron in tube *C*.

    (i)   What volume would this chlorine occupy at room temperature and pressure?

    (ii)   If this chlorine reacted completely with the iron, what mass of iron would be used up?

    (iii)   How many moles of iron(III) chloride, $FeCl_3$, would be formed?   (6 marks)

(e) It is dangerous to allow any excess chlorine left over from this experiment to escape into the room.

      (i)   Why is it dangerous to allow excess chlorine to escape?

      (ii)   How would you carry out the experiment to avoid this danger?

      (iii)   How would you detect whether the excess chlorine was escaping?   (6 marks)

(f) You have been provided with a dark solid which might be iron(III) chloride.

      (i)   Describe one test you would carry out to decide whether the solid was an iron(III) compound.

      (ii)   Describe one test you would carry out to decide whether the solid was a chloride.   (7 marks)

Figure 5.4: Stimulus question — O-level History

Question 7

Study the following statistics of selected countries in 1900 and then answer
questions (i) to (v) which follow.

	Austria—Hungary	France	Germany	Britain	Italy	Russia
Population (ms.)	45	39	56	42	32	133
Men in regular army	397,000	590,000	585,000	280,000	260,000	860,000
Annual iron & steel production (m. tons)	2.6	3.3	13.8	13.9	0.5	5.0
Annual value of foreign trade (£m.)	152	460	545	878	133	142
Merchant fleet (m. tons)	0.3	1.0	1.9	9.3	0.9	0.6
Battleships	6	23	14	49	14	24

(i)   State briefly what conclusions you would draw from:

   (a)   a comparison of Germany's population statistics with those of
          Britain and France. In what ways was the character of
          Austria—Hungary's population different from those of these three?

   (b)   a comparison of the relative sizes of the populations and the regular
          armies in the cases of France, Germany, Britain and Russia.

   (c)   a comparison in the case of all six countries listed, of the relative
          sizes of their populations and their annual statistics of iron and steel
          production.   6

(ii)   State the size, according to these figures, of the total regular armies *and*
       battleship navies, in 1900, of:

   (a)   the Triple Alliance powers

   (b)   the future Triple Entente powers   4

(iii) Show briefly what light is thrown by these statistics on Germany's anxiety
       to:

   (a)   avoid a war on two fronts

   (b)   step up the rate of her battleship construction   2

(iv) What evidence do these figures provide that Anglo—German rivalry in 1900 was industrial, maritime and commercial rather than military? 3

(v) Illustrate by reference to *one* overseas crisis, *before* 1914, how Britain and Germany confronted each other as rivals for world power. 5

Figure 5.5: Short answer question — A-level Physics

Section 1

(1 *hour*)

Answer ALL questions in this section

1.		*Steam point* $100°C$	*Ice point* $0°C$	*Room* *temperature*
	Resistance of resistance thermometer	75.000Ω	63.000Ω	64.992Ω
	Pressure recorded by constant volume gas thermometer	1.10×10^7 $N\,m^{-2}$	8.00×10^6 $N\,m^{-2}$	8.51×10^6 $N\,m^{-2}$

Using the above data, which refers to the observations of a particular room temperature using two types of thermometer, calculate the room temperature on the scale of the resistance thermometer and on the scale of the constant volume gas thermometer.

Why do these values differ slightly?   (5 marks)

2.   If a detonator is exploded on a railway line an observer standing on the rail 2.0 km away hears two reports. Why is this so? What is the time interval between these reports?
(The Young modulus for steel = 2.0×10^{11} N m^{-2}.
Density of steel = 8.0×10^3 kg m^{-3}.
Density of air = 1.4 kg m^{-3}.
Ratio of the principal specific heat capacities of air = 1.40.
Atmospheric pressure = 10^5 N m^{-2}.)   (5 marks)

3.   Show that for a person of given height standing upright the minimum length of a vertical plane mirror in which he can see his feet and the top of his head at the same time is independent of the distance between his eyes and the top of his head.   (4 marks)

4. A converging equiconvex lens of glass of refractive index 1.5 is laid on a horizontal plane mirror. A pin coincides with its inverted image when it is 1.0 m above the lens. When some liquid is placed between the lens and the mirror the pin has to be raised by 0.55 m for the coincidence to occur again. What is the refractive index of the liquid?

    (The focal length of two lenses in contact is given by $\dfrac{1}{f} = \dfrac{1}{f_1} + \dfrac{1}{f_2}$)

    (5 marks)

5. A ball is thrown vertically upwards and caught by the thrower on its return. Sketch a graph of *velocity* (taking the upward direction as positive) against *time* for the whole of its motion, neglecting air resistance. How, from such a graph, would you obtain an estimate of the height reached by the ball?   (4 marks)

6. What force is necessary to keep a mass of 0.8 kg revolving in a horizontal circle of radius 0.7 m with a period of 0.5 s? What is the direction of this force?

    (Assume that $\pi^2 = 10$.)   (4 marks)

7. A flat circular coil, with its plane horizontal, has N_1 turns and radius R_1. At its centre is a small circular coil of N_2 turns and radius R_2. When a current I flows in the large coil what is the magnetic flux through the small coil when its plane is (a) vertical, (b) horizontal? If the small coil also carries a current I what will be the couple on it when it is (c) vertical, (d) horizontal?

    (Neglect effects of the earth's magnetic field.)   (5 marks)

8. Draw a circuit diagram of a metre bridge circuit being used to compare two resistances. Why is the method only suitable for two resistances of the same order of magnitude?   (4 marks)

Figure 5.6: Short answer questions — O-level History

Examples of How to Answer the Questions

1. Which President of the U.S.A. was responsible for the introduction of the New Deal?

   Answer: *Franklin Roosevelt* (1 mark)

2. Each of these five rulers of Russia is lettered. In the answer space, arrange the five letters in their correct chronological order, starting with the earliest:

   A Alexander III
   B Nikita Khrushchev
   C Vladimir Lenin
   D Nicholas II
   E Joseph Stalin

   Answer: *ADCEB* (2 marks)

3. Complete the following paragraph:

   Gangsterism developed on a wide scale in the U.S.A. in the 1920s. An example of one of the most famous of the gangsters of that period is:

   Answer: *Al Capone* (1 mark)

4. Write a sentence to explain one of the main features of War Communism in Russia between 1917 and 1921:

   Answer: *The produce of the peasants was requisitioned by the government.*
   (2 marks)

5. Place a tick alongside the name of the President of the U.S.A. who wrote the Fourteen Points:

   ☐ Calvin Coolidge
   ☐ Herbert Hoover
   ☐ Franklin Roosevelt
   ☐ Harry Truman
   ☑ Woodrow Wilson (1 mark)

6. Underline the country with which Russia allied in 1922 at the Treaty of Rapallo:

   China   France   <u>Germany</u>   Italy   Yugoslavia (1 mark) were appraised with a view to introducing a multiple-choice component. The advantages of this form of test over the more conventional one were quickly realized. By 1974, multiple choice had been introduced into the major O-level subjects, French, History, English, Mathematics, Physics, Chemistry and Nuffield Chemistry. The advantages may be briefly summarized. Firstly, tests can be constructed to an agreed specification for both skill, knowledge, comprehension etc., and syllabus topic. Secondly, the pre-testing of items ensures that question wording is free from ambiguity and, more importantly, that the test can be constructed at an appropriate level of difficulty and discrimination. Thirdly, multiple-choice items do not require written answers (the answer is chosen from a series of five alternatives in the London system), thus enabling a fairly large number of questions and, by implication, wide syllabus coverage in a relatively short period of time. For example, the O-level History examination has 60 questions to be answered in 60 minutes. Finally, the mark gained by a candidate is simply the total number of correct answers. The marking is, therefore, objective and entirely free from subjective judgment.

A variety of types of item has been evolved to test the different types of skill. These include simple completion, multiple completion, visual negative, assertion/reason and classification. Some examples are given in Figures 5.7, 5.8, 5.9 and 5.10.

The GCE examinations of June 1974
Ordinary level examinations

At the Ordinary level, the examination generally consists of one or two written papers, the exceptions being Mathematics (three) and French (four). The duration of an examination is generally in the region of three hours. Spoken English is an exception but, since this is a paper which can only be taken by those taking English Language, it could be regarded as an extra paper. Multiple-choice tests feature in most of the examinations under scrutiny, coupled with a paper or papers requiring extended written answers of varying length and usually offering some choice of question. Incidentally, it should not be assumed that the examinations of the present and the immediate future have the same make-up. Multiple-choice tests are about to be introduced into the Biology and Geography examinations and the number of Mathematics papers is to be reduced to two.

Table 5.2 is intended to provide a summary of the characteristics of the examinations, both descriptive and statistical. The central column

Figure 5.7: Simple completion items — O-level Mathematics

Question

If $33 + 22 + 32 + 23 + 13 = 101$, to what base must the numbers be written?

A   12

B   6

C   5

D   4

E   None of the above

Key A

Question

A box contains an assortment of balls. Some are red, some are wooden and some are hollow. All the wooden balls are red. Some of the hollow balls are wooden. Which of the following statements cannot possibly be true?

A   All hollow balls are red

B   No hollow balls are red

C   Some red balls are hollow

D   All red balls are hollow.

E   Every red ball is hollow and every hollow ball is red.

Key B

Figure 5.8: Simple completion items — O-level History

Question

Pitt's Government did not grant Roman Catholic Emancipation after the passing of the Act of Union because

A   Pitt had never intended to keep his promise

B   Pitt feared the Catholics would dominate the Commons

C   George III opposed it

D   the Irish Protestants opposed it

E   the Irish Catholics wanted Home Rule

Key C

Question

'Blücher got so damnably licked that I was forced to fall back to keep my communications with him. My God, I don't think it would have done if I had not been there.'

This was said by

A   Moore about the Battle of Corunna

B   Nelson about the Battle of the Nile

C   Raglan about the Battle of Balaclava

D   Rodney about the Battle of the Saints

E   Wellington about the Battle of Waterloo

Key D

Figure 5.9: Simple completion items – O-level English Language

These questions are based on a passage which candidates had to read.

Question

Which of the following words is closest in meaning to 'blasphemous' as used in line 10?

A Indecorous

B Sacrilegious

C Barbarous

D Factious

E Obnoxious

Key B

Question

The meaning of the phrase 'persistent offensive' (line 12) may be best expressed as

A highly personal campaign

B strongly held opposition

C fiercely-mounted antagonism

D long continued abuse

E steadily continued attack

Key E

Figure 5.10: Multiple completion items — O-level Physics

Directions For each of the questions below, ONE or MORE of the responses given are correct. Decide which of the responses is (are) correct. Then choose

A	if 1, 2 and 3 are correct
B	if 1 and 2 only are correct
C	if 2 and 3 only are correct
D	if 1 only is correct
E	if 3 only is correct

Question

The resistance of a coil of iron wire is increased if

1   it is heated to red heat
2   it is placed in a strong magnetic field
3   a bar of steel is placed inside the coil

Key D

Assertion/Reason item — O-level Physics

Directions Each question below consists of an ASSERTION (statement) in the left-hand column and a REASON in the right-hand column.

Select

A   if both assertion and reason are true statements and the reason is *a correct explanation of the assertion*

B   if both assertion and reason are true statements, but the reason is *NOT a correct explanation of the assertion*

C   if the assertion is true, but the reason is a false statement

D   if the assertion is false, but the reason is a true statement

E   if both assertion and reason are false statements

Question

Assertion		Reason
If a disc is punched from a metal plate at room temperature and then both pieces are heated at 300°C, the disc will no longer fit the hole.	*because*	as the metal expands the disc gets larger but the hole gets smaller.

Key E

Table 5.2: Descriptive summary of Ordinary level examination.

Subject	Size of entry*	Multiple-choice	Short answer	Structured	Essay	Oral	Dictation	Total mark statistics M	S.D.
MATHEMATICS	Boys 9667 Girls 7378 Total 17045	1¼ hrs 33⅓%		2 hrs 33⅓% (Papers 2 and 3)				41.5	19.1
PHYSICS	11141 4300 15441	1¼ hrs 40%		2 hrs 60%				46.3	15.3
CHEMISTRY	8201 5015 13216	1¼ hrs. 40%		2 hrs 60%				58.3	18.3
BIOLOGY	7748 14847 22595		1 hr. 40%		2 hrs. 60%			45.1	16.9
GEOGRAPHY	13782 14181 27963				2 hrs 50% (both papers)			42.7	14.2
HISTORY	5905 8998 14903			2 hrs 60%				51.6	15.9
ENG. LIT. 'A'	8762 14808 23570				2½ hrs 100%			41.0	15.1
ENG. LANG.	21884 27411 49295	1¼ hrs. 35%			1¾ hrs. 65%			50.3	11.9
SPOKEN ENG.	7032 11813 18845					½ hr. 100%		59.2	13.5
FRENCH	8857 15146 24003	1 hr. 30% (Paper 2)			1½ hrs. 45% (Paper 3)	about 10 mins 15% (Paper 4)	½ hr. 10% (Paper 1)	55.5	16.2

* Figures refer to Boys / Girls / Total

classification is in terms of examining technique, the categories being multiple-choice, short-answer, structured, essay, oral and dictation. Here 'short-answer' describes questions where the response is controlled both by the form of question and the space allowed for the answer. 'Structured' questions are also directed but the answers are meant to be more extended. 'Essay' refers to the traditional, open-ended question where guidance is strictly limited. In effect, 'essay' and 'multiple-choice' sit at opposite ends of an open-closed response continuum, with 'short-answer' and 'structured' occupying intermediate positions. Within each cell of the table, information is given about the duration of papers and the percentage weighting given to each paper. Finally, in the column headed 'Total mark statistics', means (M) and standard deviations (SD) of the total marks for the complete entry are located. These marks, which are out of 100, result from combining the paper marks according to their respective weights. It is these marks which are used in the analyses in this report.

Some general observations about the contents of the table may be in order. Firstly, nowhere does multiple-choice attract more than 40 per cent of the total marks. This is in line with Board policy which makes it unlikely that any multiple-choice paper will ever attract more than 50 per cent of the total marks. Secondly, the relationship between duration and weighting is variable. A two-hour Geography paper yields only 50 per cent of the marks, while a two and a half hour English Literature paper accounts for all the marks. Having said that, it must be pointed out that it is not the Board's policy to impose a uniform relationship between duration and weighting, nor would it necessarily be desirable to do so. Thirdly, mean marks and standard deviations show considerable variation. Means range from 41.0 (English Literature) to 59.2 (Spoken English) and standard deviations from 11.9 (English Language) to 19.1 (Mathematics). The last contrast is more readily interpretable, since all our experience shows that Mathematics spreads out candidates most, while English Language spreads them least. However, as we shall see, this does not mean that English Language does not discriminate between schools. In general, total mark distributions are symmetric with a tendency to peakedness. Finally, the highest paper correlations are associated with the science subjects. Where the correlations are lower, as in English Language, it will be appreciated how the adding together of paper marks reduces the spread of total marks. It is in these subjects that there is likely to be greatest difference between the outcomes of a univariate between-school effects analysis based on total mark and a multivariate analysis using the paper marks.

For various reasons, it is the multiple-choice papers which can be described most comprehensively. Not only are the items pre-tested, but full post-examination statistics are also available. The rationale for including items consists of a blend of educational and statistical factors, with the latter ultimately carrying most force. Items with facilities less than 0.20 and greater than 0.80 are generally excluded, as are items with biserial correlations less than 0.25 (using total score on the test as the criterion). Table 5.3 provides various pieces of information about the multiple-choice tests set in 1974. Although the emphasis is on discrimination, and indeed the KR−20 figures look high, it will be seen from the standard deviations that most distributions tend towards peakedness. The reasons for this are not hard to find. These are achievement tests designed to sample broad syllabuses of work. If, as seems likely, teachers and candidates choose to sample differently and to lay greater or less stress on various parts of the syllabus, low correlations between items are bound to result; in other words, the crucial factor governing the size of the correlation is likely to be exposure to the topic in question. The difference between French and Physics is that there is no syllabus, as such, in French and the tests of reading and listening comprehension are much more obviously unitary in character and less content-based than Physics. The same argument applies to the English Language comprehension test.* What these differences imply for between-school effects is an interesting question. On the face of it, one would expect syllabus sampling to cancel out differences, also for the skill-based tests to be more sensitive to teaching and other effects associated with the school. On the other hand, there is the view of Smith (1972) that a uniform syllabus is likely to suppress differences which, by inference, may be taken to mean that syllabus sampling will amplify differences.

Before leaving the subject of multiple-choice, a word about guessing is called for. It is the Board's policy not to correct for guessing, the rationale being that candidates are best served by being invited to

---

* It is interesting that the Joint Four teachers unions, who every year collate criticisms of the London Board examinations, should report in 1974 that 'a number of schools thought that the French multiple-choice tests were more of an intelligence test than a linguistic one'. However, this was the first time such a paper had been set and these teachers may simply have been levelling a familiar accusation at multiple-choice tests out of prejudice or shock.

Table 5.3: Multiple-choice test characteristics.

Subject	Number of items	Size of entry	% finishing test	Raw score MEAN	Raw score SD	Score as % MEAN	Score as % SD	Score range	Internal consistency (KR–20)	% of items with p > .30 rb > .40
Maths	50	17045	97	26.6	8.6	53.2	17.2	1–50	.87	76
Physics	70	15441	99	36.2	9.8	51.7	14.0	4–69	.86	54
Chemistry	70	13216	99	42.4	11.5	60.6	16.4	2–70	.90	80
History	60	14903	99	33.4	9.7	55.7	16.2	1–58	.87	70
Eng. Lang.	60	49295	97	33.9	10.0	56.5	16.7	1–60	.88	60
French	45	24003	99	27.4	8.7	60.9	19.3	4–45	.89	87

attempt all questions. These are *not* speed tests and the time limits are generous, as can be inferred from the numbers finishing the tests (Table 5.3). It is accepted that candidates will use the partial knowledge at their command when in a state of uncertainty about the answer to an item. In the case of weaker candidates, this may well result in some below-chance scores. (This whole question is aired in a paper by Wood (1976) which was the basis for the Board's reaffirmation of its policy on guessing.)

So much for multiple-choice. About the measurement characteristics of the other forms of test, there is much less to be said. Unlike, for example, procedures at the Educational Testing Service (ETS), marking of essay papers is not done under what could be called controlled conditions. This is because of the tradition, not easily broken, which allows an examiner to mark in his own home at his own pace and also the difficulty of getting everyone together at the same time and for a prolonged period. The basic procedure used in most subjects, and this applies to Advanced level also, is for a briefing meeting to be held at which the chief examiners interpret the marking scheme and go through a few sample scripts. The markers then go away with their script allocations and begin marking; in English Language, the average marker would have about 600 scripts to mark in three to four weeks. On two separate occasions, early in their stint, markers are required to send in batches of 20 or so scripts to the chief examiners for their scrutiny. Should the 'chiefs' be dissatisfied with their marking, corrective action is taken. Incidentally, markers will generally work through scripts from beginning to end rather than mark one question at a time, a policy which, of course, makes the marking vulnerable to 'halo' effects.

Once the marking is completed, a standardization meeting is held at which the 'chiefs' decide, on the basis of statistics provided and their knowledge of the markers, what adjustment, if any, should be made to each marker. Among the statistics provided for each marker are centre histories, indicating how previous candidates from the schools concerned performed and, if the subject has a multiple-choice component, the distribution of the multiple-choice scores, obtained by the candidates marked by the marker. Ways of using this last information are discussed by Wood and Wilson (1974). So, although great care is taken to make the marking as fair as possible, it is not possible to give estimates of marker consistency or reliability subject by subject. Of course, 'guestimates' could be made on the basis of more or less plausible assumptions, but it is doubtful what value these would

Table 5.4: Resumé of Advanced level paper characteristics.

Subject	Size of entry*	Number of papers	Examining time (in hours)	M	S.D.	paper	1	2	3	R
Pure Maths	3334; 1778; 5112	2 (3 but only 2 are taken)	6	53.4	23.6					.87
Applied Maths	1675; 537; 2212	2	6	60.7	21.5					.83
Physics	4120; 1533; 5653	4	9½	46.2	14.4	2	.83			
						3	.63	.66		
						4	.30	.30	.37	
Chemistry	2127; 1330; 3457	3	8	42.4	13.2	2	.80			
						3	.34	.31		
Biology	1441; 2654; 4095	3	9	44.4	10.9	2	.60			
						3	.60	.53		

Table 5.4: Resumé of Advanced paper characteristics — *continued*

	N			Mean	SD		1	2	3	4
Geography	3124					1				
	3026					2	.43			
	6150	3	7	42.1	10.6	3	.35	.46		
History A	1003									
	1899									
	2902	2	6	43.3	10.7			.56		
History B	852									
	1170									
	2022	2	6	46.7	11.6			.64		
Eng. Literature	2522					1				
	6945					2	.53			
	9467	3	8½	45.9	9.6	3	.50	.49		
French	1411					1				
	4223					2	.71			
	5634	5	8	48.7	12.1	3	.54	.70		
						4	.40	.43	.40	
						5	.65	.73	.64	.41

* Figures refer to Boys / Girls / Total

have. One thing is clear. The choice element in these papers makes them less reliable than they would be if choice were to be removed.

There is little doubt that unpopular questions tend to be marked erratically because markers have little opportunity to develop a consistent marking frame. On the other hand, as Madaus and Macnamara (1970) have observed, markers tend to be stricter in their assessment of a question which has been attempted by many persons. Moreover, if most candidates answer a particular question well, markers are liable to become more and more severe as they progress through the scripts. In the English examination system, the right to question-choice is stoutly defended since it enables teachers and candidates to sample broad syllabuses in a manner congenial to their inclinations and tastes. Things are changing, however; by dint of sectionalizing papers (*e.g.*, Physics paper 1) and introducing compulsory questions, unrestricted choice is disappearing and a better balance is being struck between what might be called teaching considerations and measurement requirements. It might be noted that there are subjects, notably French and German, where everything is compulsory. These are, of course, subjects where, as was noted before, there is no syllabus as such to be sampled.

As it happens, there is some up-to-date information concerning the reliability of GCE Ordinary level examinations. Willmott and Nuttall (1975) conclude that given the restricted range of ability entered for most subjects (perhaps 40 per cent of the total population of 16 year-olds), the Ordinary level examinations are about as reliable as can reasonably be expected. Using internal consistency estimates for the various components of the examinations, and combining these into composite estimates, they report a median reliability of 0.82 for 29 subjects analyzed, the range being 0.70 (for English Language) to 0.93 (for French). They remark that people may be surprised at how high these figures are, given that most examinations are dominated by the essay type of question, generally thought to be unreliable, and suggest that 'the evidence in this report should lead to a more general acceptance of the use of essay examinations as reliable measuring instruments' (Willmott and Nuttall, 1975, p. 57).

Advanced level examinations

Since there is not the same variety of papers at Advanced level (there are no multiple-choice papers in the subjects we are considering), a table corresponding to Table 5.2 is not considered informative. Instead a resumé of the papers, together with summary statistics, is given in

Table 5.4.

As before, some general observations are in order. The average school entry for these subjects is 15 to 20. The number of papers varies from two (Applied Mathematics) to five (French), and the examining time from six hours (Applied Mathematics) to nine and a half hours (Physics). Biology, Chemistry and Physics include a practical examination. The amount of question choice permitted is, of course, more than at Ordinary level and varies from subject to subject, being greatest in History and least in French. Apart from Mathematics, correlations between papers are lower than at Ordinary level, reflecting the greater homogeneity of the candidature and (as appears likely) the increased differentiation of abilities within individuals.

There is no up-to-date information about the reliability of Advanced level examinations but the increase in papers and examining time should mean that the reliabilities are, at least, comparable with those reported at Ordinary level.

Chapter Six

Categorization and Selection of Regressor Variables and Method of Analysis

Block structure of data

The purpose of this enquiry is to examine the influence of a range of factors on pupil achievement as measured by public examinations. In considering these factors we must, on the one hand, acknowledge conceptual categories which derive from previous studies and, on the other hand, we must be prepared to acknowledge categories which derive from the particular data structure of this investigation.

Any subdivision must be preceded by a consideration of possible intrinsic structure arising from the way in which the data were collected and in this respect it is clear that we have five main sources. These are the London Examination Board, Form 7 (Schools), the school questionnaire, the teacher questionnaire and the pupil questionnaire. Since the school questionnaire and Form 7 (Schools) both yield information about the school as an institution, these two sources can be regarded as one. As far as the regression analyses are concerned, the London Examination Board yielded only information about dependent variables and so this can be regarded as one conceptual entity. For the predictor variables we have three main sources of information, these being the school, the teachers and pupils. Here we must underline the fact that for the school variables we have only one value for each school and for teacher variables we have only responses from teachers preparing students for London Board examinations and these teachers can be distinguished by the subject they teach. No further subdivision of either of these sources seems logical and so the School and Teacher blocks of data will be seen as basic conceptual units throughout the analysis. The exact content we shall discuss later.

The pupil data can be regarded in a very different light since they contain quite explicitly biographical data about the child, attitudinal data, information about the child's family and, for about one-third of the sample, the pupil's score on a verbal reasoning test prior to entering secondary school. Appropriate subdivisions of the pupil questionnaire were not easy to make but, finally, three broad divisions were decided upon. All details of the child's family would be regarded as Family variables, any attitudes which the child expressed about the school would be regarded as associated with the School and all remaining variables would be regarded as Individual Student data.

A further complication arises in the case of the pupil variables because, in contrast to the teacher and school data, each variable has a value for each candidate in a school. This clearly enables three different kinds of correlations to be computed: those between pupil variables and achievement scores in the dependent variable, those between school means for each of the pupil variables and school means for each of the dependent variables, and finally, correlations between deviations of the pupil's variables from the school means and deviations of the dependent variables from the school mean.

It was decided to run separate analyses for between-school and within-school variance. This allows each pupil variable to occur as a school mean and as a deviation score. The effect of this dual form of analysis is summarized in Table 6.1, where it can be seen that the pupil-derived variables now break up into six separate subdivisions, each with its own conceptual unity. Thus, in the between-school and within-school analyses respectively, the Family variables adopt the character of Parent Body variables and family deviation variables, the latter of which we shall simply call Family. The individual variables now become Student Body variables and individual deviation scores, the latter of which will be called simply Individual Student. Finally, the School-Individual variables, which are chiefly attitudinal in their deviation form may, in the within-school analyses, be regarded as measures of Conformity to Press.

In effect, what we have done is to divide on logical grounds the totality of data into eight separate blocks, each of which reflects some definable area of influence in the child's educational environment and which, as we shall see shortly, form subdivisions in the analyses. The blocks are Teacher, School, Parent Body, Student Body, School-Individual, Family, Individual Student and Conformity to Press. The first five of these blocks contain variables for which we have only one value for each school and are, therefore, associated solely with between-school variance. The last three blocks contain variables with one value for each pupil and are associated solely with within-school variance.

Since the number of questionnaires yielding a value of verbal reasoning score was comparatively small, it was decided to confine analyses using the variable to ones involving dependent variables which were backed by a sample of at least 300 pupils for whom verbal reasoning scores were available. This restricted the analyses to four dependent variables.

Since verbal reasoning score was a pupil variable, it was available as both a school mean and as a deviation score and, accordingly, it was decided to assign it to a separate block. Also, since the verbal reasoning score carried an age correction that could not easily be removed, it was decided to place the variable age together with verbal reasoning score into this separate block. In fact not one block but two were created; these were 'Verbal Reasoning School Mean', which is an index of the level of school intake in terms of the pupils sampled, and 'Verbal Reasoning Deviation Scores', which reflect individual performance relative to the school mean. Because of restrictions on the number of blocks which could be run in the regression programme, it was necessary to remove an existing block from the between-school runs to make room for the new one. For this reason, the Parent Body block was discarded for those analyses in which the verbal reasoning scores were used.

Selection of variables by block

The total number of variables, which were derived in a form suitable for regression analysis, came to about 200. Neither the programme nor the computing facilities were adequate to deal with this number and, in any case, it would not have been prudent to enter all items into one analysis since inspection indicated that they represented groups of heavily overlapping variables. The policy was therefore adopted of pruning the variables within each block separately in order to arrive at a short list. A complicating factor in our study, however, is the nature of our criterion variable and differences in samples associated with each criterion measure.

Table 6.1: The effect upon pupil-derived variables of division into school means and deviation scores.

	Original variable group		
	Family	*Individual*	*School–Individual*
Between-School analysis	Parent Body	Student Body	School–Individual
Within-School analysis	Family	Individual Student	Conformity to Press

One of the features of the study is the breadth of different measures of achievement which are used as criteria. Unfortunately, however, the pupils taking any particular subject at O-level or A-level were a self-selected group and, although we include 11 subjects at O-level as criteria, no single pupil will have taken all 11 subjects; in general a pupil may be expected to have taken from three to six subjects. Therefore, in examining the different topics taken at O-level, we are concerned with different populations of pupils who may have markedly different characteristics.

Conventional wisdom suggests that these differences would be greatest between the Arts and Science based students who will take few examination papers in common and may be expected to display different attitudes towards their schools. Although, in many respects, it would have been convenient to work with a single correlation matrix calculated on the total pupil sample and including all 11 O-level subjects, given the small degree of overlap among pupils taking certain subjects (*cf.* Table 6.2), this could hardly be justified. At the very least it would have been calculated on the whole sample, whereas correlations between predictors and dependent variables should relate only to the sample corresponding to each dependent variable. There is no guarantee that correlations between predictors calculated in this way would be truly representative of relationships between predictors for each of the subsamples taking a given subject.

Because correlations were calculated using only complete pairs of values, additional problems would arise in the use of a single correlation matrix. This becomes clear if, for example, we consider the dependent variable, Biology, and the predictor variable, age. In calculating the correlations, the co-variance term will include only those pupils for

Table 6.2: Numbers of pupils in the total sample taking two O-level subjects.

	Chemistry	Maths D	Physics	Eng. Lang.	Eng. Lit. A	French	German	History B	Geography	Sp. Eng.
Biology	245	308	233	863	544	692	233	369	607	677
Chemistry		198	329	346	223	350	108	148	257	267
Maths D			299	472	357	414	139	167	352	302
Physics				387	225	366	117	175	304	290
Eng. Lang					843	1084	418	549	973	1164
Eng. Lit. A						755	259	313	591	486
French							425	496	806	730
German								198	288	287
History B									354	455
Geography										663

whom we have both a Biology score and an age score but, in calculating the variance term, the variance over all Biology scores will be used and likewise, the variance of all ages in the pupil sample will be used. If it occurred, for some reason, that the ages of pupils taking Biology were drawn from a narrow stratum of the total age sample, then the variance term used in the calculation would be incorrect and would give rise to a wrong estimate of correlation between age and Biology.

Having assigned the variables to blocks on a conceptual basis, it was now possible to begin the selection of variables within blocks. This involved the use of a step-wise regression method, in which each dependent variable was regressed on the variables within each block separately. This was done for each of the eight blocks, with the 11 dependent variables at O-level, which involved carrying out 88 separate regression analyses, and with the four dependent variables at A-level, involving a further 32 regression analyses. In the case of both Ordinary and Advanced level, additional analyses were carried out for the total sample taking examinations at a given level in which students' attitude to school was the dependent variable. In the analyses involving students' attitude, it should be noted it was not possible to use variables in the Teacher block as predictors, since teacher variables are subject specific, and so, when the total student sample is aggregated, as was the case for the attitude analyses, the teacher variables have no meaningful interpretation. Variables derived from the teacher questionnaire relating to teacher attitudes were, however, included in the School block and, in this context, were run against students' attitude as a dependent variable.

The same list of variables as had been used in the analyses using total variance was at first used in the analyses of between-school variance for O-level subjects. However, after the first complete runs of the regression analyses and partitioning of variance had been completed, it became apparent that unacceptable negative values of unique contribution of blocks to variance had been permitted to occur. This had happened despite the use of the careful procedure described below.

When the separate regression analyses for each block were completed, a print-out of variables in the order in which they had been selected was obtained, together with statistics relating to the contribution of the variables to the explanation of variance and their associated F-values. This list of variables was inspected and variables which did not contribute to the explanation of variance at the five per cent level of confidence, at least, were deleted. Attention was then directed to the contribution to explained variance of those variables which were above the significance level and which were admitted to the regression equation. The nature of step-wise regression is such that at each step, the variable making the largest possible contribution to explained variance is selected and so, if the procedure behaves correctly, the contribution of each successive variable should decline. Correspondingly, one expects the F-values to decline in a smooth and reasonable manner. Unfortunately, when regression analysis is run with a small number of degrees of freedom, as was the case most particularly on the between-school runs, the process capitalizes on high correlations in the matrix. This leads to an inflation of the explained variance and, on occasions, the effect can be sufficiently severe to induce into the step-wise procedure an instability. This is immediately evident when a reversal in the trend of the contribution made by successive variables appears. Thus, instead of finding a steady decline in the amount of variance explained, a reversal occurs, and successive variables explain increasing amounts of variance until 100 per cent is reached. Since this phenomenon is largely due to high correlations between pairs of predictor variables, one of the manifestations of the difficulty is the presence of a high and negative product of R and Beta. Such a variable is sometimes known as a suppressor variable but, in this particular context, its role is much more severe than that of mere suppression.

When this instability was witnessed, it became necessary to identify the possibly offending variable, remove it from the list of predictor variables and re-run that regression analysis before operating the selection procedure. This was necessary in about ten per cent of the between-school runs. Unfortunately there is no guarantee that the same problem will not occur when blocks of variables are jointly entered into the regression and, in fact, it did happen that negative values appeared in the final tables. The offending negative unique contributions to variance by block had arisen because of between-block interaction of variables and it was, therefore, necessary to apply a similar strategy to that used for the separate analyses of blocks. The pruning that was necessary was severe and markedly altered the relative contributions to variance. Data in tables provided in this book are derived from the 'pruned' data. Time and resources did not permit the same procedure to be adopted for student attitude as a dependent variable, nor for the A-level and verbal reasoning score analyses.

In the case of the Ordinary level examinations, a second series of analyses was conducted using the verbal reasoning test data. This was not carried out for the Advanced level because of an insufficiency of students in the sample and, at Ordinary level, the sample was only adequate in the cases of four subject variables. In the case of O-level, however, since the use of the verbal reasoning test merely involved the addition of an extra block containing the verbal reasoning test scores and student's age, it was not judged to be necessary to make a new selection of predictor variables for these analyses. It is true that the student sample in each of the analyses using verbal reasoning score was smaller than that in the use of corresponding subjects without verbal reasoning score, but any predictive effects which are subject-specific are assumed to be represented in the selection made upon the larger sample. The procedure, therefore, was to adopt those variables which had already been selected for the relevant subjects, to remove the variable AGE from the Individual block (which was only selected in the case of Biology) and to enter it and verbal reasoning score into the same new block.

In the following sections we shall discuss the selection of variables during the preliminary sorting process on a block by block basis. Within the discussion on each block, we shall present both the Ordinary and Advanced level selections beginning with the Ordinary level. The general character of the variables that are selected within each block will be discussed. The tables will be presented in the following order for each block separately. The first table will contain the full list of variables available for inclusion in the analysis. The variables will be listed here as they apply to the O-level results and the reader should note that the same list applies to the A-level, with the exceptions of variable 7, OLVLTOT, which becomes ALVLTOT, meaning the total number of papers taken by the student in the relevant examination and variable 6, SAPASS (student's self-assessment) which in the case of A-level adopts the number 8. The second table contains a list of the independent variables selected for further analyses at O-level. In the table, the association of an independent variable with a dependent variable is indicated by a plus or minus sign. This sign indicates the sense of the zero-order correlation between the relevant predictor and dependent variable and is a useful indication of the consistency of behaviour of a predictor variable. The third table in each block discussion contains the subset of predictor variables which was selected in the A-level analyses.

Teacher Variables

All of the variables in the Teacher block are derived from the teacher questionnaire and, in the analysis, all are expressed as school means. In the case of each dependent variable, only data from teachers who teach to the appropriate examination level are included in analyses, and a mean is derived from that sub-sample of teachers within each school. This implies that in many subjects, the number of subject teachers will be very few and, in practice, variations range from zero to five subject teachers. In cases where we have no subject teacher, this implies that for some reason the questionnaire was not returned.

The teacher variables entered are listed in Table 6.3 and comprise some 31 items. Of these, most represent biographical data and must, therefore, be regarded as status variables, while some 14 are process variables associated with teaching style. These 14 variables are divided into two groups of seven. The first group deals with different kinds of lesson management, while the second group deals with types of mechanical aids. Teaching methods which involve the use of lectures, discussions and writing periods in the classroom clearly involve a considerable degree of overlap and, although attempts were made to factor analyse these variables, the result was not marked with any success, partially due to the small sample of schools and partly because of the subject-specific nature of some of the styles. For example, it is to be expected that practical periods will be singularly associated with science subjects and that field trips will be mainly confined to those subjects involving environmental observation such as Biology, Geography and, to a lesser extent, some of the Arts subjects. There are similar difficulties associated with the variables dealing with mechanical aids, and in the case of some items, the response to the variable is clearly an indication of resource availability. This is particularly notable in the responses to the use of a slide projector or film-strip projector, which inspection of the source data seems to indicate is a school-specific item; again, in the use of the overhead projector, one may be seeing the results of school policy in equipping particular subject areas with this facility. The two variables concerned with whether the teacher adapts his teaching method to suit group differences or individual differences may perhaps be regarded as true process variables but, once again, the responses will inevitably be influenced by practices which are peculiar to certain subject areas, as for example in laboratory science work, when the use of small working groups and partnerships may be particularly common.

Table 6.3: Teacher variables.

Code name	Variable number	Variable description	
YREXP	169	Length of teaching experience in months	
TRAIN	170	Was teacher trained in subject being taught	NO/YES
WKTM	171	Number of terms spent in preparation	
RVTM	172	Number of weeks spent on revision	
BTGP	173	Adapts teaching to group differences	NA/NO/YES
BTIND	174	Adapts teaching to individual differences	NA/NO/YES
OTHESUB	175	Has taught another subject to 'O' level	NO/YES
SAMESUB	176	Has taught same subject to 'O' level before	NO/YES
LECTURE	177	Uses lecture method	Never/Sometimes/Often
DISCUSS	178	Uses discussion method	Never/Sometimes/Often
WRITE	179	Has writing periods	Never/Sometimes/Often
DICTATE	180	Dictates lesson notes	Never/Sometimes/Often
PRACT	181	Practical periods are used	Never/Sometimes/Often
FIELD	182	Field trips	Never/Sometimes/Often
PROJ	183	Uses project work	Never/Sometimes/Often
TV	184	Uses T.V. transmissions	Never/Sometimes/Often
FILM	185	Uses films	Never/Sometimes/Often
RADIO	186	Uses radio	Never/Sometimes/Often
TAPE	187	Uses tape recorder	Never/Sometimes/Often
SLIDE	188	Uses slide projector	Never/Sometimes/Often
STRIP	189	Uses film strip projector	Never/Sometimes/Often
OHEAD	190	Uses overhead projector	Never/Sometimes/Often
HMWK	193	Homework expectation in hours	
PRIV	194	Private study expectation in hours	
PSTEXER	195	Uses past exam papers for timed exercises	Never/Sometimes/Often
PSTGUID	196	Uses past exam papers as guide to syllabus	Never/Sometimes/Often
YRSHERE	206	Years at current school	
YRSTOT	207	Total years teaching experience	
QUAL	208	Qualification: Increasingly Academic on a 5 point scale	
TSEX	209	Teacher's sex	Male/Female
TAGE	210	Age group on a 9 point scale	

In each case the value occurring last has the highest numerical value in the regression analysis.

The variable concerned with teachers' qualifications was coded with a degree of misgiving in accordance with a notional scale which confounded a variation from vocational to academic with an increasing duration of teacher education. It may be that this variable is a proxy for an approach to learning which is characteristic of different kinds of higher institution. Be that as it may, we found that in the case of six out of the 11 O-level subject variables, qualification is selected as making a significant contribution to the explanation of variance.

Table 6.4 lists the teacher variables which were selected to go on to further analysis at the O-level and Table 6.5 lists those variables which were selected at the A-level. The first striking feature of Table 6.4 is the apparent lack of consistency among dependent variables and those predictors which they select. Only three variables from the entire list attain the distinction of being selected by four or more dependent variables; these are the 'amount of time spent preparing for the examination' (WKTM), the 'use of discussion type lessons' (DISCUSS) and 'teacher's qualification' (QUAL). Of the subject variables, Chemistry is notable in selecting only three predictors of significance while Spoken English is notable in selecting nine such predictors. No other clear patterning is observable and it seems that we are faced with a series of variables with a very high degree of overlap. In this context, it will be recalled that, whereas selection depended primarily on achieving sufficient significance in their contribution to explained variance, some variables were eliminated because they provoked instability in the regression process. At the A-level, a smaller number of variables survive the screening process and there is little difference between subject variables in the number of predictor variables selected. The range of selected predictor variables is wide, covering teacher background, teaching process and the use of mechanical aids.

School variables

The situation with regard to the school variables is a little more complicated because of the variety of sources of information which contribute to this block. In the main, the variables are contributed by the school questionnaire with additional details from Form 7 (Schools) and one or two special additions by the coding staff which refer to school location. Table 6.6 presents the complete list of school variables and it will be noted that among them are some variables with the comment 'Not Entered'. This arises because of the procedure for entering dummy variables into a regression analysis. An example is the

Table 6.4: Teacher variables selected for between-school analysis indicated by sign of simple r (O-level).

Code name	Variable number	BIOLOGY	CHEMISTRY	MATHS D	PHYSICS	ENG. LANG	ENG. LIT A	FRENCH	GERMAN	HISTORY B	GEOGRAPHY	SP. ENG.
YREXP	169	+			−	+						
TRAIN	170	+		+								
WKTM	171					+				−	+	+
BTGP	173	+										
BTIND	174					−						
OTHESUB	175				−	−						
SAMESUB	176							+				
LECTURE	177				−							
DISCUSS	178	+				+	+			+		
WRITE	179	−					−					−
DICTATE	180								+			−
PRACT	181					+	+	−				
FIELD	182						+					
PROJ	183	−										
TV	184							+			+	+
FILM	185							−			+	+
RADIO	186							+			+	
TAPE	187											+
SLIDE	188						−					
STRIP	189									+		
OHEAD	190				−							+
HMWK	193										−	+
PRIV	194										−	+
PSTEXER	195				−							
YRSHERE	206		+									
YRSTOT	207							−				
QUAL	208		−	+		+		+	+		+	
TSEX	209				−							

Table 6.5: Teacher variables from the long list selected for between-school analysis, indicated by sign of simple r (A-level).

| Teacher variables | | Criterion measures | | | |
| | | PURE MATHS | ENG. LIT | FRENCH | GEOGRAPHY |
Code name	Variable number				
YREXP	169		+		
TRAIN	170		−		
WKTM	171	+			
BTGP	173	−		+	
DICTATE	180				−
PROJ	183	+		+	−
TV	184		−		

Table 6.6: School variables.

Code name	Variable number	Variable description	
DIRGRANT	90	School is Direct Grant	
MAINTAIN	91	School is L.E.A. Maintained	
INDEPENDENT	−	School is Independent (not entered)	
HOUSES	92	Has a formal house structure	
YEARS	93	Has a year structure coarser than single years	
DOMAUT	94	Above divisions have autonomy for domestic purposes	
ACAD	95	Above divisions have autonomy for academic purposes	
PHOUSES	96	Pupils would perceive a House structure	
PYEARS	97	Pupils would perceive a Year structure coarser than single years	NO/YES
LABS	98	Number of labs compared with mean of the sample	LOW/HIGH
AVAS	99	Audio visual aids compared with sample mean	
COUNS	100	Has a guidance counsellor	NO/YES
O/EXAMS	101	Proportion of 'O' levels to all exams at 14+	
EXAMS	102	Total number of 'O' level and C.S.E. offered	
SUBREST	103	Exams restrict school syllabus	NO/YES
ADMISS1	104	Admission Factor 1 (Academic criteria)	+
ADMISS2	105	Admission Factor 2 (Interview rather than test results)	−
DENOMF	106	Religious denomination is a factor in admitting a pupil	NO/YES
SEXPF	107	Sex of pupil is a factor in admitting a pupil	NO/YES

Table 6.6: School variables *cont'd*

Code name	Variable number	Variable description	
CONSULT	108	Should parents be consulted on academic matters	OTHER/YES
SES	109	Head's estimate of school SES. 5 point scale.	Working-class high
STR1	110	Degree of mixed ability years 1, 2, 3.	Mixed is high
STR2	111	Degree of mixed ability years 4, 5	Mixed is high
STR3	112	Degree of mixed ability year 6	Mixed is high
POPUL	113	Urban or Rural environment	Rural/Urban
SIZE	114	Number of pupils on register	
SSEXM	115	School is all boys	NO/YES
SSEXF	116	School is all girls	NO/YES
SMIXED	—	School is mixed (not entered)	
PTRATIO	117	Size divided by number of teachers	
MTEACH	118	Proportion of male teachers	
PTRAT14	119	Pupil-teacher ratio at exam age	
PUPIL16	120	Number pupils mainly 16 and over	
LEA1	121	Sample L.E.A. 1	NO/YES
LEA2	122	Sample L.E.A. 2	NO/YES
LEA3	123	Sample L.E.A. 3	NO/YES
LEA4	—	Sample L.E.A. 4 (not entered)	
MODERN	124	School is Secondary Modern	NO/YES
GRAMMAR	125	School is Grammar	NO/YES
COMPREHEN	126	School is Comprehensive	NO/YES
DIR & INDEP	—	Direct Grant and Independent (not entered)	
TOPIN1	155	Opinion of all teachers Factor 1 (Study important to all)	—
TOPIN2	156	Opinion of all teachers Factor 2 (Focus of study upon exams)	+
TOPIN3	157	Opinion of all teachers Factors 3 (Exam performance more important than study)	+
TOPIN4	158	Opinion of all teachers Factor 4 (Concern with pupils as individuals)	+
DAY	211	School has entirely day pupils	NO/YES
BOARD	212	School has entirely boarding pupils	NO/YES
MIXED	—	School has day and boarding pupils (not entered)	
AEXAMS	213	Total number of A level subjects offered by school	
ADMISS3	215	Admission Factor 3 (Family Preference)	+
ADMISS4	216	Admission Factor 4 (Advertise, Day, Geographic catchment)	—
ADMISS5	217	Admission Factor 5 (Neighbourhood criteria)	+

In each case the value occurring last has the highest numerical value in the regression analyses.

Table 6.7: School variables selected for between-school analysis indicated by sign of simple r (O-level).

School variables — Code name	Variable number	BIOLOGY	CHEMISTRY	MATHS D	PHYSICS	ENGLISH LANG	ENGLISH LIT A.	FRENCH	GERMAN	HISTORY B	GEOGRAPHY	SP. ENG.
								Criterion measures				
MAINTAIN	91	−			−			−		−		−
LABS	98			+								
O/EXAMS	101					+	+				+	
EXAMS	102					−						
ADMISSI	104		+		+							
SES	109						−					
STR1	110		+									
STR2	111		−				+			−		
SSEXM	115					+					+	
SSEXF	116			−								
PT RATIO	117						−					−
MTEACH	118					−				+		
PUPIL16	120			+					+		+	+
TOPIN1	155	−										
TOPIN2	156										+	
AEXAMS	213							+				
ADMISS3	215				−		−					
ADMISS4	216									−		

Table 6.8: School variables selected for between-school analysis indicated by sign of simple r (A-level).

School variables		Criterion measures				
Code name	Variable number	PURE MATHS	ENG. LITERATURE	FRENCH	GEOGRAPHY	ATTITUDE
DIRGRANT	90	+				
YEARS	93		−			
PHOUSES	96				+	
O/EXAMS	101				+	
POPUL	113			−		−
SSEXM	115					−
MTEACH	118			−		
PUPIL16	120	+				
LEA3	123					−
GRAMMAR	125				−	
COMPREHEN	126	−			−	
TOPIN1	155		−			
TOPIN2	156		−			
TOPIN4	158			−		
AEXAMS	213				+	

case of school type, where the categories Direct Grant, Maintained and Independent are mutually exclusive. Here only the first two categories were entered into the regression equation, each coded in a dichotomous manner; the third variable was omitted since its value was implied by the remaining two.

Also among the school variables is a group of four which are contributed by the teacher's questionnaire. These relate to a question which was common to both teacher and pupil questionnaires. The variables derived from this question are coded as TOPIN1 to TOPIN4 and are concerned respectively with 'the importance to students of studying', 'the importance of study as a means to achievement in exams', 'the importance of examination results rather than study' and finally a general factor, 'concern with all pupils as individuals'. The factor analysis was performed upon the total sample of teachers without regard to subject and the four variables used here are factor scores derived from the responses of all sample teachers in each school. We shall see that in the case of the pupil questionnaire, the pupil responses are scored in relation to these four factors defined by the teachers. It is also of significance that these four variables are among the very few in the school variable list which can be regarded as process variables. Other possible contenders as process variables are the second factor derived from the admissions procedures which is concerned with 'the importance of interviews with parents and pupils rather than with academic results' (ADMISS2) and the variable which records whether the principal teacher thinks parents should be consulted on academic matters (CONSULT).

Tables 6.7 and 6.8 show those school variables which contribute sufficiently to explanation of variance to be admitted to further analysis in the case of O-level and A-level respectively. Once again, we see the same scattered responses in terms of predictor variables selected, which was evident in the case of teacher variables. A few exceptions to this observation stand out. One is type of school. At the O-level, five dependent variables select a school type designation (MAINTAIN) as being significant. At the A-level, a number of variables relating to type of school (Grammar and Comprehensive) also survive the screening process.

Parent Body and Family variables

These variables are derived from the pupil questionnaire and relate to his home environment. They are listed in Table 6.9. There are only

Table 6.9: Family variables.

Code name	Variable number	Variable description	
FAEDU	28	Father's Education relative to child	Longer/Same/Shorter
MAEDU	29	Mother's Education relative to child	Longer/Same/Shorter
FAJOB	31	Social Class of Father's job	Working class high
FAMPACE	37	Family sets pace. Mean of ranks for siblings and parents	Less pace set high
HMHELP	39	Members of family give help	No/Yes
JOBCMP	89	Mean of comparisons with father's job, child's job	Less/Same/More

In each case the value occurring last has the highest numerical value in the regression analyses.

E

Table 6.10: Family variables selected for between-school and within-school analysis indicated by sign of simple r (O-level).

	Code name	Variable number	BIOLOGY	CHEMISTRY	MATHS D	PHYSICS	ENG. LANG.	ENG. LIT. A	FRENCH	GERMAN	HISTORY B	GEOGRAPH	SP. ENG.
PARENT BODY	FAEDU	28					−		−				−
	MAEDU	29									−		
	FAJOB	31	−	−	−		−	−	−			−	
	HMHELP	39	−	−			−						
PARENT	FAEDU	28		−		−		−	−			−	
	MAEDU	29	−	−		−	−	−	−	−	−	−	−
	FAJOB	31									−		−
	FAMPACE	37						+				+	
	JOBCMP	89	+		+			+	+	+	+	+	

Table 6.11: Family variables selected for between-school and within-school analysis indicated by sign of simple r (A-level).

	Code name	Variable number	PURE MATHS	ENG. LITERATURE	FRENCH	GEOGRAPHY	ATTITUDE	
PARENT BODY	FAEDU	28			−	−		
	MAEDU	29	−					
	FAJOB	31	−		−			
	FAMPAGE	37		+		+		
	HMHELP	39		−			+	
	JOBCMP	89	+					
PARENT	MAEDU	29	−		−			
	FAMPACE	37				+		
	HMHELP	39		+			−	

six such variables, the first three of which were derived directly from questions on the pupil questionnaire relating to the education and employment of parents. The next two questions were derived indirectly from pupil responses and indicate to what extent the family acts as pace-maker for the student's work. The two variables in question are coded FAMPACE, a low score on which indicates that the family sets the pace and HMHELP which indicates whether or not the family helps with homework. The sixth variable of this group is an unfortunate combination of student responses about whether or not the job he aspires to has more or less of certain attributes. The attributes, as such, have no easily identified collective characteristics because of the way in which they were coded but response to this question can be expected to indicate a degree of dissonance between the job to which the child aspires and that which the father holds.

Bearing in mind that all of these variables are used for both the Parent Body and Family blocks, we may examine in what respects their characteristics are modified by being used as school means or as deviation scores. For instance, Table 6.10 indicates that, in terms of school means, the first two variables, level of father's education and level of mother's education, tend to be selected with a degree of mutual exclusion while in terms of deviation scores, the tendency is for both of these parental characteristics to be selected. What may be happening here is that the level of academic attainment in the parental body is indicated by the parent with the higher score, so one or other parent is a sufficient indicator of this status. In contrast, it seems that the presence of an individual parent with a particular academic standing does not seem to pre-empt the predictive power of the education of the other parent with respect to individual differences in achievement.

Student Body and Individual Student variables

Like the Family variables, the Student Body and Individual Student variables are also derived from the pupil questionnaire and, because they relate exclusively neither to family circumstances nor to the school, they are attributed to the students, either individually or collectively. In the form of school means, they comprise the Student Body variables and, as deviation scores, they are the Individual Student variables. Table 6.12 contains the complete list of variables and Tables 6.13 and 6.14 the selected variables for O and A-level subjects respectively. Only two of the variables, AGE and SEX, are truly situational. The remaining variables are largely attitudinal and adopt

Table 6.12: Individual Student variables.

Code name	Variable number	Variable description	
AGE	4	Child's age in months	
SEX	5	Child's sex	Male/Female
SAPASS	6	Mean of self assessment in all subjects. 5 point scale	Good pass is high
OLVLTOT	7	Total O-level exams sat by child	
ATTITUDE	25	Attitude to leaving school	'Anything to stay' high
STATUS	26	How bright are you. 5 points	Least bright is high
ASPIRE	27	Academic aspiration. 5 points	University is high
JOBASP	30	Job aspiration. 5 points	Working class high
TCHEXP1	32	Pupil view of teacher expectation in best subject	At bottom is high
TCHEXP2	33	Pupil view of teacher expectation in worst subject	At bottom is high
IPACE	34	Rank order of self pacing	Less pace set high
FRSPACE	35	Rank order of friends' pacing	Less pace set high
TMSTUDY	38	Hours per week studying	Less pace set high
PRHELP	40	Parents help with work	No/yes

Table 6.13: Student variables selected for between-school and within-school analysis indicated by sign of simple r (O-level).

	Code name	Variable number	BIOLOGY	CHEMISTRY	MATHS D	PHYSICS	ENG. LANG.	ENG. LIT. A	FRENCH	GERMAN	HISTORY B	GEOGRAPHY	Sp. ENG.
STUDENT BODY	AGE	4	−			−							−
	ATTITUDE	25		+	+	+			+		+		
	FRSPACE	35				−			−				
	TMSTUDY	38	+	+		+	+				+	+	+
	PRHELP	40						+					
INDIVIDUAL STUDENT	AGE	4	−				−		−				
	SEX	5	+			−	+	+	+				
	SAPASS	6	+	+	+	+	+	+	+	+	+	+	+
	OLVLTOT	7			+		+	+	+	+	+	+	
	ATTITUDE	25										+	
	STATUS	26	−	−	−	−	−	−	−	−	−	−	
	ASPIRE	27	+	+		+	+	+	+		+	+	+
	JOBASP	30	−	−	−							−	
	TCHEXP1	32	−				−	−	−	−			−
	TCHEXP2	33	−	−		−			−		−		
	IPACE	34	−				−					−	
	FRSPACE	35	−		−		−					−	
	TMSTUDY	38	+				+	+				+	+

Table 6.14: Student variables selected for between-school and within-school analysis to serve as Student Body and Student variables (A-level).

| | Individual Student variables | | Criterion measures | | | | |
	Code name	Variable number	PURE MATHS	ENG. LIT.	FRENCH	GEOGRAPHY	ATTITUDE
STUDENT BODY	SEX	5					+
	SAPASS	8	+	+		+	
	ALVTOT	62	+	+			
	ATTITUDE	25			+		
	ASPIRE	27			+		
	JOBASP	30					−
	TCHEXP1	32	−				
	TCHEXP2	33	+		−		
	IPACE	34		+			
	FRSPACE	35	−			−	+
	TMSTUDY	38				+	−
	PRHELP	40					−
INDIVIDUAL STUDENT	AGE	4			−		
	SAPASS	8	+	+	+	+	+
	ALVTOT	62	+	+			+
	STATUS	26		−	+		
	ASPIRE	27				+	
	TCHEXP1	32		−	−		
	TCHEXP2	33	−	−			
	IPACE	34					+

very different aspects, depending on the way in which the scores are used; the only variables among these which denote process are 'time spent on study' and 'parents help'.

As a Student Body variable, AGE is selected at O-level, but not at A-level. It is selected as an Individual variable at both levels. In all instances, the sign of r is negative indicating that increased age is associated with lower achievement, both in terms of school means and the performance of individuals. Inspection of the correlation matrix shows that this direction of association is consistent for all subjects in the between-school situation and for most subjects in the within-school matrix.

The variable, SEX, presents some problems because of the composition of the sample. Our schools were entirely boys', entirely girls', or mixed with a ratio very close to 50 per cent. As a variable, SEX was not selected for the Student Body block for any dependent variables, with the exception of Attitude at A-level. Within-school variation, of course, is only possible in the case of mixed schools. Being a boy in such a school at O-level is associated with high achievement in Biology, English Language, English Literature and French, whilst being a girl is associated with high achievement in Physics. SEX is not selected as a variable for the Individual Student block at A-level.

A number of variables purport in one way or another to be estimates of a pupil's likely success in the examination. Some of these are attitudinal variables and some are indices from school-related situations. The first (SAPASS) is a score derived from the pupil's estimate of his chances of success over all the examination subjects he is taking. That is to say, the aggregate of his estimate of success is taken for all O-levels in the case of O-level analyses and for all A-levels in the case of A-level analyses. This variable turns out to be a frequently selected predictor at both examination levels; it is selected for the Individual Student block by all dependent variables. OLVLTOT is the total number of O-level papers being taken by a student. It might be expected that the number of papers taken by a student, which is largely determined by the school's assessment of his success, would give some indication of the student's academic ability and indeed, this variable turns out to be a reasonably powerful predictor, being selected as a positive indication for most of the dependent variables. The equivalent variable at A-level (ALVTOT) survives in the case of two of the four subject areas.

The variable derived from the question 'How bright do you think you are' (STATUS) is coded in such a way that the response lowest in the class is coded with a high score. At both O and A levels, and particularly at the former, STATUS is selected as a predictor for the Individual Student block. The selection indicates that individual students within a school who have a high opinion of themselves tend to be high achievers within the school. The relatively frequent selection for the Individual Student block of the variables TCHEXP1 (which is the response to the question 'How able does your teacher think you are in your best subject) and TCHEXP2 (which is the response to the question relating to the student's view of his teacher's expectation in his worst subject,) provides additional evidence on the relationship between perceptions of students' achievement and their actual achievement in examinations. The selection of these variables indicates that pupils who perceive their teachers as having a high opinion of them — in their good subjects as well as in their weak subjects — are high achievers.

The estimate by the student of his academic aspirations (ASPIRE) also correlates with achievement and is selected by the Individual Student block for a high proportion of dependent variables at O-level. The estimate of students' job aspiration (JOBASP) is also selected within the Individual Student block. Once again, the coding is such that negative correlation indicates that high job aspiration goes with high achievement. With one exception, these variables do not appear as predictors in the Individual Student block at A-level.

Given these patterns of relationship, one might have expected the variable, ATTITUDE, which indicates the student's attitude towards school, to be frequently selected for both Student Body and Individual Student blocks. At the Student Body level, the variable is indeed selected in the case of five dependent variables at O-level and one at A-level. For those variables, the data indicate that achievement tends to be higher in schools where the pupils indicate contentment with staying on at school. By contrast, Attitude is notable by its failure to be selected for the Individual Student block, except in the case of O-level Geography. However, an examination of the correlation matrix indicates that it is positively correlated with achievement within schools, the correlation with all subject variables being significant at the one per cent level. Most likely, the non-selection of Attitude for the Individual Student block indicates that, in the regression analyses, other variables with which it is correlated have pre-empted the variance they hold in common with it.

Variables associated with a student's method of work survive for some subjects. One of these indicates that the student is aware of being paced by himself (IPACE), the other that he is paced by his friends (FRSPACE). The variables, for the most part, appear in the Individual Student rather than in the Student Body block and they behave with reasonable consistency: where self-pacing, or being paced by friends appears, it is associated with high achievement. The variable relating to time spent studying (TMSTUDY) is selected for many dependent variables in both the Student Body and the Individual Student blocks; the more time spent studying, the higher the achievement of student and student bodies. As far as parental help to the student (PRHELP) is concerned, we see that it is selected only in the case of English Literature for the Student Body block.

School-Individual and Conformity to Press variables

All of the variables in this section are derived from the pupil questionnaire and arise from attitudes which the pupils expressed about their schools (Table 6.15). In the questionnaire, the emphasis of the questions is upon the pupil's view of the ethos of the school and the kinds of pressures which it exerts through teaching and disciplinary processes. The first group of seven items in this section relates to the factor analysis of questions on both the pupil questionnaire and the teacher questionnaire relating to attitudes to examination and learning (Table 4.3). As has already been indicated, the scores for these four variables are derived by taking the pupil's response scaled on the factor coefficients of the teachers' responses. Thus, the pupil's score indicates a pupil opinion within a conceptual framework defined by the teacher.

When the scores in this section are expressed as school means, we clearly have opinions of the student body in each school about that school, and this may be regarded as a good index of the perception of school press felt by the pupils within a school. In the case of deviation scores, however, we are observing the differences between a pupil's perception of press and the perception of press of the entire student body and this may be regarded as an index of conformity to press.

The variable, SOPIN1, which relates to the perception of a school as traditional and conservative in behaviour and academic matters, is selected by a number of dependent variables in both the School-Individual and the Conformity to Press blocks, particularly at the O-level (Table 6.16). The positive direction of the relationship indicates that schools perceived as traditional and conservative tend to

Table 6.15: School—Individual variables.

These are variables which can be assigned to individuals but are manifestly attributable to his interaction with the school. All are derived from pupil opinions about the school and are entered as factor scores. The sign indicates the sense in which the described attribute is scored.

Code name	Variable number	Variable description	
SOPIN1	18	School is traditional and conservative in behaviour and academic matters	+
SOPIN2	19	School has a reputation for academic success	−
SOPIN3	20	School emphasizes good habits and self-expression	−
SOPIN4	21	School is relatively unstructured and rule free	−
SOPIN5	22	School is intolerant of and tends to alienate the less academic pupils	
SOPIN6	23	School emphasizes hard work and acceptance of given material	+
SOPIN7	24	Emphasis on sport and adaptability to the student makes school enjoyable	−
OPIN1	41	Study is important to all pupils	+
OPIN2	42	The main focus of study is upon examinations	−
OPIN3	43	Examination performance is more important than study for its own sake	+
OPIN4	44	The school has concern with pupils as individuals	+

Table 6.16: Opinion variables selected for between-school and within-school analysis indicated by sign of simple r (O-level).

	Code name	Variable number	BIOLOGY	CHEMISTRY	MATHS D	PHYSICS	ENG. LANG.	ENG. LIT. A	FRENCH	GERMAN	HISTORY B	GEOGRAPHY	SP. ENG.
SCHOOL–INDIVIDUAL	SOPIN1	18					+	+		+			
	SOPIN3	20			+	+	+					+	+
	SOPIN5	22	+				+					+	+
	SOPIN6	23		+			+					+	
	SOPIN7	24							−	−			
	OPIN1	41	−			−			−		−		−
	OPIN2	42					+	+	+				
	OPIN3	43		+			+					+	+
CONFORMITY TO PRESS	SOPIN1	18	−					−	−		−		
	SOPIN2	19		−	−	−	−			−	−		
	SOPIN5	22	−				−	−	−	−	−		
	SOPIN6	23					+						
	SOPIN7	24											+
	OPIN1	41			+		+						
	OPIN2	42	+				+						

be high in achievement. The negative signs in the Conformity to Press blocks may indicate that, within schools, pupils who perceive the school as being other than traditional and conservative tend to be low achievers. The correlation matrix, however, indicates that the negative relationship between Conformity to Press and achievement is very small and fails to achieve significance in any case.

The variable, SOPIN2, which relates to the school's reputation for academic success, in the case of the School-Individual block appears only at A-level and there the pattern of relationships is inconsistent. The variable also appears in the Conformity to Press block at O-level; here the relationship is consistent, indicating that those students who are aware of the good academic reputation of the school, tend to be high achievers. The school's emphasis on good habits and self-expression (SOPIN3) is selected as a predictor for a number of dependent variables in the School-Individual block, but is not selected for any school subject in the Conformity to Press block. The direction of selection indicates that emphasis on good habits and self-expression tends to be associated with low achievement.

At O-level, the variable SOPIN5 is selected for four of the dependent variables in the School-Individual block and for seven of the variables in the Conformity to Press block. This factor deals with intolerance of less academic pupils leading to alientation. The data indicate that schools, in which the student body perceives this intolerance, tend to be high achieving schools but that pupils who perceive this intolerance tend to be low achievers. The pattern at A-level is similar, though here the variable is selected only once for the School-Individual block and twice for the Conformity to Press block.

The variable, SOPIN6, which indicates an emphasis on hard work and acceptance of given material, is selected for a few variables in the School-Individual block at both O and A-levels and the direction of relationship indicates that schools with this emphasis tend to be associated with low achievement. The variable is selected by only one dependent variable in the Conformity to Press block, and that is at O-level. A variable relating to sport and the adaptability of the school to a student and to the school making life enjoyable (SOPIN7) appears a few times in the School-Individual block and once in the Conformity to Press block. It appears only at O-level. At the between-school level, the relationship is such that schools which emphasize sport and adaptability are associated with low achievement. Within schools, in the case of the one dependent variable which selects this predictor, the

Table 6.17: Variables selected for between-school and within-school analysis to serve as School—Individual and Conformity to Press variables (A-level).

	Code name	Variable number	PURE MATHS	ENG. LIT.	FRENCH	GEOGRAPHY	ATTITUDE
					Criterion measures		
SCHOOL—INDIVIDUAL	SOPIN1	18					−
	SOPIN2	19	−		+		−
	SOPIN3	20	+				
	SOPIN4	21	−	−	−	−	
	SOPIN5	22				+	
	SOPIN6	23		+			
	OPIN1	41				−	+
	OPIN2	42		+		+	
	OPIN4	44					+
CONFORMITY TO PRESS	SOPIN1	18		−			
	SOPIN3	20					−
	SOPIN5	22	−				−
	OPIN1	41			+		
	OPIN2	42	−				−
	OPIN4	44		−			

direction of the relationship is such as to indicate that high achievers in Spoken English perceive an enjoyable sporting atmosphere in the school.

The view that 'study is important to all students' (OPIN1) appears in the School-Individual block for five examination subjects at O-level and for one at A-level. This variable also survives in the Conformity to Press block, for two subjects at O-level and for one at A-level. The directions of the relationship are consistent. Schools which emphasize the importance of study for all students tend to be associated with high achievement but, within schools, pupils who perceive this feature tend to be low achievers.

Emphasis on study for examinations is also associated with high achievement. The relevant variable (OPIN2) appears with three variables at O-level and two at A-level in the School-Individual block and with two variables at each level in the Conformity to Press block. Further evidence that emphasis on examination performance is consistent with high achievement is to be found in the association of the variable OPIN3 (examination performance is more important than study for its own sake) with four dependent variables at O-level in the School-Individual block.

Method of analysis: Decomposition of variance

Having assigned variables to blocks, the final analyses of data were carried out. These, too, used the multiple regression technique. Student achievement, as measured on the separate GCE examinations, were the dependent variables in the analyses. Blocks of independent variables served as regressor variables. In the programme used, provision was made for a maximum of five blocks to be entered and for all possible intersections of those five blocks to be explored. The precise sets included depended on whether the analysis was concerned with between-school variance or within-school variance. In the between-school analyses, the relevant blocks were Teacher block, School block, Parent Body block, Student Body block and School-Individual block. In the within-school analyses, the blocks employed were Family block, Individual Student block and Conformity to Press block.

A number of earlier studies (*e.g.*, Coleman *et al.*, 1966) employed a model in which the school variables were entered into regression equations after home background factors had been entered. This procedure has certain disadvantages; in particular, it provides no estimate of the overlap that may exist between school and other variables. For the present study the analytic model used is very similar to that suggested by Mood (1969) and employed by Mayeske *et al.*, (1972) in their reanalysis of the Coleman data. The main advantage of this model is that it partitions the variance in the dependent variable, which can be attributed to independent variables or blocks of independent variables, into unique and common components.

Perhaps the simplest way to explain the relationship between components of variance is through the use of a Venn diagram. In our analyses we shall be dealing with 'blocks' of variables, that is, sets of variables which have been grouped according to rational and/or empirical criteria. For the purpose of illustration, three blocks will be considered. One is a Family (F) block, in which the variables measuring characteristics of the pupil's parents or home are entered. A second block is an Individual (I) one, in which are placed those variables which measure characteristics of the individual pupil. The final block is a Conformity to Press (C) one; variables which characterize the student's perception of school ethos and the kinds of pressure it exerts on him are placed in this block.

The Venn diagram in Figure 6.1 represents the partitioning of explained variance in a dependent variable into seven mutually exclusive components.* The sum of the variance explained by each of these seven components equals the total amount of variance in the dependent variable explained by the Family, Individual and Conformity to Press blocks. In the diagram, the area labelled U(F) represents the amount of variance in the dependent variable uniquely explained by variables in the Family block. This explained variance in the U(F) component is mutually exclusive of that explained by the other six components. The area labelled U(I) represents the amount of variance in the dependent variable uniquely explained by variables in the Individual block. The area labelled U(C) represents the amount of variance uniquely explained by the variables in the Conformity to Press block. The Comm (FI) component represents the amount of explained variance attributable jointly and solely to Family and Individual blocks. The Comm (FI) component is also mutually exclusive of the U(F) and U(I) components. Explained variance that is jointly shared between two

---

* A disadvantage of the use of Venn diagrams to illustrate the partitioning of variance is that they cannot portray negative commonalities which can occur as a result of negative regression weights or sampling errors in the correlation matrix (*cf.* Creager, 1971).

Figure 6.1: Venn diagram for partitioning of variance.

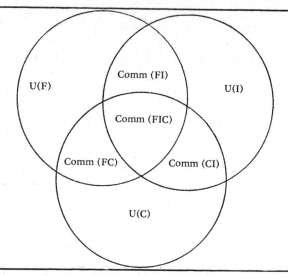

Figure 6.2: Equations for estimating components of variance.

1. $R^2(F)$ = U(F) + Comm(FI) + Comm(FC) + Comm(FIC)
2. $R^2(FI)$ = U(F) + Comm(FI) + Comm(FC) + Comm(FIC) + U(I) + Comm(CI)
3. $R^2(FIC)$ = U(F) + Comm(FI) + Comm(FC) + Comm(FIC) + U(I) + Comm(CI) + U(C)
4. $R^2 I$ = U(I) + Comm(FI) + Comm(CI) + Comm(FIC)
5. $R^2(CI)$ = U(I) + Comm(FI) + Comm(CI) + Comm(FIC) + U(C) + Comm(FC)
6. $R^2(C)$ = U(C) + Comm(FC) + Comm(CI) + Comm(FIC)
7. $R^2(FC)$ = U(C) + Comm(FC) + Comm(CI) + Comm(FIC) + U(F) + Comm(FI)

8. U(C) = $R^2(FIC) - R^2(FI)$
9. U(F) = $R^2(FIC) - R^2(CI)$
10. U(I) = $R^2(FIC) - R^2(FC)$

11. Comm(FI) = $R^2(FC) - R^2(C) - U(F)$
12. Comm(FC) = $R^2(CI) - R^2(I) - U(C)$
13. Comm(CI) = $R^2(FI) - R^2(F) - U(I)$

14. Comm(FIC) = $R^2(F) - U(F) - Comm(FI) - Comm(FC)$

blocks is called commonality. Thus the area labelled Comm (CI) represents the commonality of the Conformity to Press and Individual blocks, exclusive of all unique components associated with the Family block. Likewise, the area labelled Comm (FC) represents the commonality of the Family and Conformity to Press blocks, exclusive of any other component in the diagram. Finally, the component in the diagram labelled Comm (FIC) is the commonality among all three blocks exclusive of the other six components.

Figure 6.2 provides equations which were used in determining the estimates for the partitioning of variance into unique and shared components. Equation 1 represents the multiple correlation squared (R^2) when the predictor variables are from only the F block. This R^2 equals the sum of the unique component for the F block and all commonalities associated with it. Equation 2 represents the multiple correlation squared when the predictor variables are from the F and I blocks. R^2 in equation 2 equals the sum of the unique component for the F block, the unique component for the I block and all commonalities associated with blocks F and I. Equation 2 differs from equation 1 in that it includes the unique component of the I block and the commonality of the I and C blocks. Equation 3 represents R^2 when the variables from all three blocks are in the equation. This multiple correlation equals the sum of all three unique components and of all their commonalities. Thus equation 3, in addition to giving us everything that equation 2 contains, adds the unique component for block C. Hence, the difference between equation 3, and equation 2 yields the unique component for block C, which is specified in equation 8. Equations 4 and 6 are similar to equation 1, in that they refer to R^2 for a single block. Equations 5 and 7 are similar to equation 2 in that they refer to R^2 for two blocks. From these seven equations all components for partitioning of the variance explained by the three blocks can be calculated.

The remaining seven equations specify the procedures utilized to derive the estimates in the partitioning of the variance. Each of the unique components is estimated by the difference between a multiple correlation squared for all of the blocks and the appropriate multiple correlation squared involving two blocks. Thus, the unique component for block C equals the R^2 for all three blocks minus the R^2 for blocks F and I. The commonalities involving two blocks equal a two-block R^2 minus a one-block R^2 and a unique component. For example, the commonality for the F and I blocks equals the R^2 for the F and C blocks together, minus the R^2 for the C block and the unique component for the F block. The final commonality to be estimated is for the overlap of all three blocks. This commonality is equal to the R^2 for the variables in the F block minus the unique component for the F block minus the commonality for the F and I blocks and minus the commonality for the F and C blocks. Thus all seven components are estimated via the differences in the seven multiple correlations and other components.

Chapter Seven

Results of GCE Examinations: Between- and Within-School Variance

As has already been noted, the sample of students returning survey questionnaires and therefore incorporated in the regression analyses was an incomplete, self-selected sample which differed for each of the subject examinations taken. In order to obtain some estimate of the representativeness of this sample, analyses were carried out specifically for this study by the London Examinations' Board on the examination results of all students attending school in the Local Authority areas from which schools had been sampled for the main study. This group of students completely embraces the sample for whom data were obtained for the regression analyses of the present study. Questionnaire data were not, of course, available for the students included in the analyses carried out by the London Examinations' Board.

As well as providing estimates of the representativeness of our sample, these analyses also throw some light on variations in achievement between schools. Such analyses have limitations since they neither take into account differences in school resources nor how student populations might have differed on entry to school. However, analyses which focus on *subject-wise* between-school variation and, through the multivariate analyses, on differences associated with papers or, more generally, testing techniques and tasks are, by virtue of being comparative, free, to some extent, of the criticism. Some schools will be superior in all departments but if they excel particularly in one department, this surely has implications in terms of differential exploitation of resources.

We shall first of all present results of the analyses of variance as carried out by the London Examinations' Board. This will be followed by the results of similar analyses based on the examination results of the survey sample selected for the present investigation. The two sets of results will be compared.

London Examinations' Board analyses
Ordinary level examinations

Using the MULTIVARIANCE package (Finn, 1972), a one-way analysis of variance or, what amounts to the same thing, a discriminant analysis based on total mark was carried out. The left side of Table 7.1 presents, for each subject considered, number of schools (k), number of candidates (N), the ratio (N/k), mean square within-school variance (MSW), mean square between-school variance (MSB) — these last two rounded off —, the F-ratio, $\hat{\omega}^2$, which provides an estimate of the magnitude of the school effects and $\hat{r}_{ic}$, the intraclass correlation, which serves the same purpose. As a matter of fact, and as the values in the table suggest, these two statistics are not very different. The formula for estimating ω^2 is

$$\hat{\omega}^2 \quad = \quad \frac{(k-1)(F-1)}{(k-1)(F-1) + N}$$

The basic formula for r_{ic}, assuming for the sake of the argument equal numbers in each of the k schools, is

$$\hat{r}_{ic} \quad = \quad \frac{MSB - MSW}{MSB + (k-1)MSW}$$

This can be written in terms of F as

$$\frac{F-1}{F+k-1}$$

which in turn can be expressed in the form

$$\hat{r}_{ic} \quad = \quad \frac{(k-1)(F-1)}{(k-1)(F-1) + k(k-1)}$$

The only difference between this form and the expression for $\hat{\omega}^2$ is the difference between N and k(k−1) or k^2. For most subjects, at both levels, the values of N and k^2 turn out to be quite similar.

Table 7.1: Between-school analysis, univariate and multivariate: O-level. (Total sample of students taking London Board examinations in four areas.)

Subject	N Pupils	k Schools	N/k	MSW Within variance	MSB Between variance	F	$\hat{\omega}^2$	$\hat{r}_{ic}$	F_{mult}	P1	P2	P3	P4	$\hat{\omega}^2_{mult}$
					Univariate						Multivariate Paper F values			
Biology	2733	58	47	176	2322	13.15	.20	.17	13.95	13.10	13.52			.39
Chemistry	1613	44	37	271	3728	13.78	.25	.23	8.55	12.64	13.54			.27
Mathematics D	2278	46	50	262	6005	22.88	.30	.32	8.71	21.33	19.78	20.56		.37
Physics	1827	53	35	182	1936	10.65	.22	.15	7.66	11.17	8.07			.31
English Language	6025	83	73	97	3018	31.12	.29	.27	18.97	27.36	22.07			.36
English Literature A	2957	52	57	156	2504	17.97	.23	.25						
French	3442	58	60	187	3147	16.79	.21	.21	10.81	13.47	14.30	11.17	14.57	.38
History B	2065	44	47	118	1301	11.07	.17	.19	9.01	11.05	9.89			.28
Geography	3577	65	55	158	2382	15.12	.20	.18	19.30	21.21	12.30			.44
Spoken English	3049	46	66	125	2086	16.69	.19	.25						

Coming now to the interpretation of Table 7.1, it is clear, whichever measure of relationship is relied on, that the strongest school effects are associated with Mathematics and English Language and the weakest with Biology, Physics, History and Geography, with French and Chemistry occupying intermediate positions. Although final judgment must be withheld until the results of the multivariate analysis are studied, this is still a somewhat surprising outcome. It has been generally assumed that between-school differences are likely to be largest where, as Lindquist (1966) puts it, 'the opportunity to learn what is tested is relatively restricted to the classroom and to the formal school curriculum, and to be least where the achievement measured might more often result from out-of-school experiences and informal learning' (p.271). It is true that secondary school Mathematics is essentially a formal body of knowledge and techniques and so might be said to fit into the first category but there is little doubt that English Language falls fairly and squarely into the latter category. Admittedly, the skills called for — writing an essay, doing a précis and demonstrating comprehension in answers to multiple-choice items — are not so obviously susceptible to home effects as say, reading or vocabulary, but of all the subjects in the curriculum this is the one which seems least school-dependent.

What is striking about the English Language results is the small within-school variation — an error standard deviation of ten points on a 100-point scale. Evidently, performance within schools is very homogeneous. Mathematics, on the other hand, has almost the largest within-school variation yet, because the between-school variation is so great, it still shows the biggest effect. We therefore have the situation where the subjects with the largest and smallest between-student differences in terms of total mark produce the biggest between-school differences. However, it should not be overlooked that English Language, certainly, and Mathematics to a lesser extent, are subject to less ability-related entry selection than other subjects such as Physics, Chemistry and French, which attract high calibre entries. If all schools aimed to select and enter a certain ability band for a particular subject and were more or less successful, even though some would have more eligible pupils than others, then one might argue that one would not expect to find much between-school variation.* Interference of this

---

* One could also argue, however, that the achievement of such homogeneity among students would more readily permit the demonstration of school and teacher effects.

kind may well be present in these data, although its existence in no way invalidates any differential of paperwise school effects which may emerge from the multivariate analysis, the details of which are now considered.

Before presenting any results, a brief gloss on the statistics and their interpretation is necessary. When evaluating the results of a one-way multivariate analysis of variance, what matters in the first place is the size of the multivariate F-value. Providing they are significant, the univariate F-values associated with the various papers can be interpreted; if not, they ought to be ignored. To measure the strength of school effects, multivariate analogues of ω^2 and r_{ic} are available along with other possible measures, all of which are functions of the roots of the characteristic equation (*cf.* Joe and Anderson, 1969; Porebski, 1966). To keep matters simple we prefer to use the multivariance analogue of ω^2, ω^2_{mult} (Sachdeva, 1973).

When interpreting values of ω^2_{mult}, it must be borne in mind that they are measures of the *maximum* strength of relationship it is possible to get, achieved by assigning to paper scores those weights (technically, the standardized discriminant coefficients) which maximize differences between schools. Instead of total paper scores arrived at by weighting positively in the usual way, we get new composites called canonical variates. Being a multivariate analysis, there are as many of these as there are significant dimensions of achievement along which schools differ, with the proviso that the number of dimensions cannot exceed the number of variables or papers. The upshot is that interpretation of ω^2_{mult} and measures like it must be looked upon as a rather theoretical exercise. If, in practice, paper scores were to be weighted according to the optimum formula, schools would not necessarily emerge as being maximally different since they would presumably re-direct their efforts to correspond with the new weighting scheme, making the outcome hard to predict. Were it to be the case, as often happens, that the weighting formula for the first and most important dimension took the form $W_1 X - W_2 Y$ then schools would be placed in a peculiar position, since presumably they would feel obliged to ignore paper Y completely and concentrate entirely on Paper X. The message to be drawn from all this is that most attention should be paid to the profiles of mean paper scores and especially to contrasts within these profiles.

The right side of Table 7.2 shows the results of the multivariate analysis for the Ordinary level data. There are no results for English

Literature and Spoken English because these are single paper examinations. All multivariate F values and univariate values too, are highly significant. Mathematics and English Language are as prominent as before but the big change concerns Biology and Geography and, to a lesser extent, French, all of which now show strong school effect. The classification of Physics, History and Chemistry as showing the weakest school effects is more or less confirmed.

Why Biology and Geography? The answer is that both subjects discriminate quite strongly between schools and individuals along two dimensions. This is in contrast to Mathematics which discriminates very effectively but only along one dimension, a result, which, of course, stems from the high correlations between papers. Subjects like Physics and History on the other hand, discriminate along two dimensions but fairly weakly. With French, the situation is that on no dimension does it discriminate strongly but there are four significant dimensions and therefore more information in the statistical sense.

At the individual paper level, there are no remarkable results. The notion that multiple-choice papers might be less sensitive to school factors than essay-type papers is not really borne out to any extent. In Physics and English Language, the pattern of results (univariate F-values) points in this direction but in Chemistry and Mathematics the reverse pattern occurs. (P2 is the multiple-choice paper in all cases except Mathematics where it is P1.) It may be, however, that the inclusion of a multiple-choice paper in the History examination has reduced the between-school variation from what it would have been otherwise.

Advanced level examinations

At Advanced level (Table 7.2), there is again a conflict between the univariate and multivariate results. Biology and Applied Mathematics stand out as extremes in both sets of results but what of French, Geography and History A?

Compared with the Ordinary level results, it will be observed that the univariate $\hat{\omega}^2$ values are lower, while the $\hat{\omega}^2$ mult values are higher. The reason for this has a lot to do with the number of papers. Given more papers and lower correlations between them, the total mark is bound to be less sensitive. On the other hand, the more papers, the more dimensions and the greater $\hat{\omega}^2$ mult is likely to be. This helps to explain the discrepancy in the results for History A and, in a different way, French and Physics. All the same, one thing is clear from these

Table 7.2: Between-school analysis, univariate and multivariate: A-level. (Total sample of students taking London Board examinations in four areas.)

Subject	N Pupils	k Schools	N/k	MSW Within variance	MSB Between variance	F	$\hat{\omega}^2$	$\hat{r}_{ic}$	F_{mult}	P1	P2	P3	P4	P5	$\hat{\omega}^2_{mult}$
												Paper F values			
Biology	400	25	16	81	818	10.12	.35	.27	9.71	5.25	15.63				.74
French	469	29	16	121	380	3.15	.11	.07	4.95	6.76	2.66	2.84	6.09	2.29	.73
Geography	665	39	17	72	376	5.23	.19	.10	4.22	6.20	3.80	4.31			.47
Pure Maths	486	25	19	477	2331	4.89	.16	.13	3.29	4.60	4.78				.23
Applied Maths	145	10	15	424	633	1.49	.03	.05	1.99	1.62	1.57				.17
Physics	548	26	21	137	619	4.51	.14	.12	6.37	4.20	3.44	3.30	15.42		.64
Chemistry	302	17	18	153	809	5.30	.19	.20	3.81	4.49	4.98	4.02			.41
History A	290	18	16	93	555	5.94	.22	.22	4.83	5.15	5.77				.37
History B	179	11	16	109	151	1.38	.03	.02	5.16	3.00	2.77				.38
English Literature	1050	46	23	69	264	3.82	.11	.06	5.51	3.38	4.54	6.20			.46

results: the effects associated with English and Mathematics are not nearly so great relative to other subjects as at O-level. This we should expect, since the examination populations are much more selective. With Biology, however, it appears that an exception must be made.

Of all the papers studied, it is the Biology practical which discriminates most effectively between schools. Several reasons for this come to mind. Practicals are more susceptible to intensive coaching with the commensurate pay-off in results. The time a teacher spends on practical work may be more a function of his tastes and inclinations than the time he spends on theory work. Having said that, it should follow that theory papers should also show strong school effects but this is not the case. No doubt, extra time spent on practical work produces a better yield. Schools will also vary in the excellence of their facilities and the extent of ancillary help. In this connection, it may be significant that the Joint Four criticisms of the 1974 Biology examination should mention that 'teachers would appreciate questions which do not require hours of preparation beforehand (especially as some schools do not have laboratory technicians)'.

What has been said about Biology might equally well be said about Physics, although, in this case, the net effect is not so marked because of the lower weight the Physics practical receives and the lower correlation it exhibits with the other papers. Why the Chemistry practical should not show more variation is hard to say; perhaps the nature of the task allows less latitude for gaining advantages in preparation, both academic and logistic.

Before leaving this question the impact of differential selection ought again to be mentioned. Biology is one of the Advanced level subjects which attracts a wider range of ability and so is more likely to register between-school variation. That does not alter the value of discovering that the variation is registered most strongly in the practical.

Analyses for survey sample

The magnitude of between-school variation, examination by examination, for the survey sample is reported in this section. The results of the one-way analyses of variance for Ordinary level subjects may be found in Table 7.3 and for Advanced level subjects in Table 7.5. The examination subjects listed for the O-level are the same as those used in the analyses described in the last section (Table 7.1), with two exceptions; German and a measure of attitude, which occur in the

Table 7.3: Between-school analysis of variance: O-level.

Dependent variable	Total variance	Within variance	Between variance	F	ω^2	Estimated proportion within	N Pupils	K Schools
Biology	223.72	170.67	1828.02	10.71	.2374	.7629	1061	35
Chemistry	334.92	247.83	2263.2	9.13	.2607	.7400	461	21
Maths D	406.01	235.26	4826.0	20.51	.4207	.5794	618	24
Physics	264.33	177.88	1942.24	10.92	.3356	.6730	550	28
Eng. Lang.	149.82	94.74	3047.31	32.16	.3677	.6324	1929	37
Eng. Lit. A	175.84	166.92	524.41	3.14	.0515	.9492	1064	28
French	247.80	179.20	3172.5	17.70	.2836	.7231	1351	32
German	222.34	183.47	957.41	5.22	.1760	.8252	494	26
History B	147.38	117.92	1260.89	10.73	.2034	.7974	648	18
Geography	194.20	146.45	1751.49	11.96	.2462	.7541	1208	37
Spoken Eng.	152.37	121.52	1837.46	15.12	.2029	.7975	1165	22
Attitude	1.942	1.746	12.031	6.89	.6874	.9126	2643	44

present analyses, were not included in the analyses reported in the last section. In the case of the A-level examinations, the results for fewer subjects were available for the survey sample than had been available for the analyses in the last section — four examinations (Table 7.5) as against ten (Table 7.2). Since statistics comparable to those presented in the last section are presented in this section, comparisons may be made between findings based on the larger sample and findings based on the survey sample for those examinations which are common to the two sections.

A comparison of Tables 7.1 and 7.3 indicates that the extent of the sampling for the survey ranges from roughly half the pupils for Biology to rather more than quarter of the pupils in the case of Mathematics. The proportion of schools sampled shows rather less variation, ranging from about 40 per cent for History to 60 per cent for Biology.

Furthermore, it can be seen from a comparison of the tables that while the within-variance and the F-values are much the same, the values of $\hat{\omega}^2$ are, with a few exceptions, higher for the smaller sample. In most cases, the increase is in the order of 20 per cent. This is because in each subject the numbers in the survey sample have shrunk to about one-third, whereas the number of schools has only reduced by half. Rewriting the formula for $\hat{\omega}^2$ as

$$1 - \frac{1}{1 + (F - 1)/(^N/k - 1)}$$

the effect of any reduction (or increase) in the average number of pupils per school, given that F remains constant, becomes clear. The exception is English Literature, where the value of omega squared changes from .23 in the large sample to .05 in the smaller survey sample. The most likely explanation for the large discrepancy appears to be a preponderance of girls' schools in the survey (reduced) sample, English Literature being a subject in which girls out-perform boys, making it likely that school differences will be sex-related.

Table 7.4 presents the corresponding analysis of variance results for those subjects which were analyzed in conjunction with verbal reasoning test scores. Only in the case of four subjects was the number of pupils for which we had a verbal reasoning score in excess of 300. (A number less than this was regarded as inadequate for the present purpose.) Here we see much more dramatic changes in the value of F and of omega squared, both of which are more than can be attributed to the change in sample size. Part of the reason, no doubt, is that verbal

Table 7.4: Analysis of variance for samples with verbal reasoning scores: O-level.

Dependent variable	Total variance	Within variance	Between variance	F	ω^2	Estimated proportion within	N Pupils	K Schools
Biology	194.97	160.31	890.16	5.55	.1686	.8314	359	17
Eng. Lang.	148.02	94.96	2016.2	21.23	.3458	.6542	689	19
French	238.00	199.80	1278.3	6.40	.1497	.8502	368	13
Geography	184.46	138.50	1157.9	8.36	.2502	.7498	375	18

Table 7.5: Between-school analysis of variance: A-level.

Dependent variable	Total variance	Within variance	Between variance	F	ω^2	Estimated proportion within	N Pupils	K Schools
Pure Maths	597.24	521.39	1249.57	2.397	.1264	.8735	193	21
Eng. Lit.	75.01	59.383	369.25	6.673	.2237	.7763	374	20
French	153.82	123.06	453.32	3.684	.2024	.7976	201	20
Geography	100.85	68.211	432.52	6.340	.3248	.6752	211	20
Attitude	1.9597	1.6779	12.9082	7.693	.1445	.8555	832	22

reasoning test scores are only available in the case of Maintained schools and so both Independent and Direct Grant schools are excluded from the sample. In the cases of Biology, English Language and Geography, the number of schools sampled is reduced to about half the number available for the main analysis while in the case of French it is reduced to nearly a third. For all subjects, the number of pupils is reduced to about a third of the number in the main analysis. All the F-values for these sub-samples are considerably depressed and all the values of omega squared are also depressed, with the exception of Geography where the value has increased fractionally. The conclusion is inescapable that the subsample for whom verbal reasoning test scores was available is not representative of the main sample and this must be borne in mind when comparing the results of the regression analyses on this subsample with those on the main sample.

For the Advanced level examinations, a very different kind of picture emerges as comparison of Tables 7.2 and 7.5 illustrates. The first thing to note is that the sample of students has dropped in size to about a third of that available for the analyses reported in the last section, while the number of schools is perhaps 30 per cent lower, although subject to large variation. Here the first sign that the survey sample is no longer representative is given by the large change in F-values, in the case of Pure Mathematics from 4.9 to 2.4, for English Literature from 3.8 to 6.7, for French from 3.2 to 3.7, and for Geography from 5.2 to 6.3. What we see here is a sample of schools in which the response proportion is sufficiently small to impose serious errors on the school means. Why this low response rate occurred, and whether it entailed a degree of self-selection which has conspired to inflate the F-value is unclear, but it does indicate that a note of caution must be sounded in interpreting the regression analyses, particularly those concerned with between-school effects. We also note from Table 7.5 that the values of omega squared tend to be inflated, as compared with those in the London Examinations' Board analyses, once again indicating a larger between-school component of variation than exists in the larger sample.

Conclusion

In this chapter, we examined the representativeness of our sample by comparing statistics derived from the sample with statistics derived from the population of all London Board GCE examinees attending school in the four Local Authority areas from which the schools had been sampled for our study.

Comparisons indicate that the extent of sampling at the O-level ranges from about half the pupils for Biology to a little more than a quarter in the case of Mathematics. The proportion of schools sampled shows rather less variation, ranging from about 40 per cent for History to 60 per cent for Biology. A further reduction in size may be noted for the sample for which verbal reasoning test scores were available. The size of this sample reduces to between a third and a half, depending on subject, of the sample available for the main analyses.

At the A-level, the sample of students for our main analyses is made up of about one-third of examinees taking A-level examinations in the four Local Education Authorities from which our sample was drawn. The number of schools is about 30 per cent lower, though there is considerable variation by subject.

When one looks at the values of other statistics, one sees that the reductions in sample size were accompanied by other changes. In particular, the value of omega squared is larger for the smaller sample, indicating a larger between-school component of variation in the smaller as compared to the larger sample. The situation is somewhat different for the still smaller sample of students for whom verbal reasoning scores were available; for two of the four subjects on which analyses were carried out, the value of omega squared was depressed by comparison with values obtained on the other two samples. At the A-level, the tendency was for the value of omega squared to be inflated for the smaller as compared to the larger sample.

As well as providing information on our sample, the findings in this section may be used as a basis for some comments on between and within-school variations in achievement. In his recent critique of the school effects literature, Coleman (1975a) drew the general conclusion that the relative strength of school and extra-school influences is subject-specific. All the results of our analysis point in the same direction. As to which subjects are most susceptible to school influences, Lindquist's (1966) belief that between-school differences are most likely to occur where the opportunity to learn what is being tested is relatively restricted to the classroom finds no great support, plausible though it is; indeed it might be said to be self-evident. Whether the fact that these classroom-based subjects are most likely to experience ability-related entry selection and that this is responsible for obscuring the differences is impossible to say, although it must exert a fairly powerful effect. At any rate, it is the basic subjects in the curriculum, which most 16-year olds capable of tackling GCE Ordinary level attempt — English Language and Mathematics, particularly the former — which produce the greatest between-school variation.

When it comes to Advanced level, naturally all subjects experience greater selection, some more than others. It is perhaps no accident that one of the subjects which attracts a broader ability entry, Biology, should show the greatest between-school variation, although the fact that this variation manifests itself chiefly in the practical examination suggests that the cause is directly connected to the exploitation of school resources and to variations in teachers' enthusiasm for practical work. That Physics, a more restricted entry subject, should produce the same result is further evidence for this view. It is also true that another of the less selective entry subjects, Geography, shows no pronounced between-school variation.

Chapter Eight

Results of Regression Analyses and Partitioning of Variance

In this chapter, we report the results of analyses designed to determine how much variation in achievement exists between students within a school and how much exists between schools in mean achievement. Secondly, we seek to determine how much of these variations can be accounted for by measurable factors in the circumstances of individuals and schools. Our measures of achievement throughout are the subject examinations for the General Certificate of Education, 11 in all at the Ordinary level – Biology, Chemistry, Mathematics, Physics, English Language, English Literature, French, German, History, Geography and Spoken English, and four at the Advanced level – Mathematics, English Literature, French and Geography. So as not to limit ourselves entirely to cognitive measures, a measure of attitude to school, derived from data supplied by individual students in a questionnaire, was also included as a measure of school output. Information on the circumstances of individuals was obtained from a number of sources – questionnaires completed by students, teachers and headmasters as well as a form returned by schools to the Department of Education and Science (Form 7) (Schools). The relationships between this information (which forms the basis of our independent variables) and our measures of school outcome (dependent measures) are determined in our study by the use of regression analysis.

Results of regression analyses

We have already referred to the way in which the data entered into the regression analyses were structured by blocks and the variables subsequently sifted block by block to yield subsets to be entered into the final regression analyses. The school-mean variables concerned with between-school effects were represented by five blocks: Teacher, School, Parent Body, Student Body and School-Individual. Similarly, the deviation scores concerned with within-school effects were represented by the blocks, Family, Individual, and Conformity to Press. To obtain an overall appreciation of the extent to which variance in the criterion variables can be explained, we shall consider the results which are yielded by aggregating all of the school mean blocks and all of the deviation score blocks. Assuming that omega squared leads to a correct estimate of the variance attributable to between-school effects, we shall go on to estimate what proportion of total variance is explained respectively by the school-mean blocks and the individual blocks and subsequently add these figures to obtain an estimate of the proportion of total variance which is explained by all predictors.

A. *Ordinary level examinations*

The results of analyses using O-level subjects as dependent variables are presented in Table 8.1. Columns 1 and 2 indicate the proportions of variance attributable to between-school and within-school effects respectively. Column 3 indicates the proportion of the between-school variance which can be accounted for in the regression analyses. Similarly, column 4 indicates the proportion of within-school variance accounted for. Both sets of figures are taken directly from the final summary print-out of each composite regression analysis and are not corrected for degrees of freedom nor are they pruned to eliminate non-significant variables from the final regression equations. The extent to which this slightly inflates values will be discussed later.

Each figure in column 5 is the product of the figures in the same row in columns 1 and 3; likewise, the figures in column 6 are the products of figures in columns 2 and 4. The column 5 figures indicate the proportion of total variance in the criterion variable which is explained by the between-school and within-school regression analyses respectively. Column 7 is formed by summing the figures in columns 5 and 6 and represents the proportion of total variance which is explained by both the between and within-school regression analyses together.

One may note that of the between-variance, the greater part, in fact between 67 per cent in the case of Biology and 99 per cent in Chemistry, can be explained by school mean predictors. Bearing in

Table 8.1: Composition of explained variance: O-level.

Dependent variable	ω^2	Estimated proportion within	Explained between	Explained within	Explained between of total	Explained within of total	Total explained
Biology	.2374	.7629	.6700	.3119	.1591	.2379	.3970
Chemistry	.2607	.7400	.9852	.4810	.2568	.3559	.6127
Maths D	.4207	.5794	.8618	.2728	.3626	.1581	.5207
Physics	.3356	.6730	.9128	.4097	.3063	.2757	.5820
Eng. Lang.	.3677	.6324	.9091	.2744	.3343	.1735	.5078
Eng. Lit. A	.0515	.9492	.7829	.2940	.0403	.2791	.3194
French	.2836	.7231	.9608	.3196	.2725	.2311	.5036
German	.1760	.8252	.9767	.3130	.1719	.2583	.4302
History B	.2034	.7974	.7186	.2989	.1462	.2383	.3845
Geography	.2462	.7541	.8580	.3007	.2112	.2268	.4380
Spoken Eng.	.2029	.7975	.8732	.0777	.1975	.1618	.3593
Attitude	.0874	.9126	.7143	.2623	.0624	.2394	.3018

F*

mind that the predictors entering this equation have already been sifted from a much longer list, this represents a situation in which we have an over-abundance of data capable of predicting the level of school means achieved on each of the criterion variables. But in terms of proportion of total variance which can be predicted by between-school factors, the limiting consideration is not the power of the predictors but the amount of variance which exists between schools. This is demonstrated in column 5 where, as we saw, the product of columns 1 and 3 represents the proportion of total variance explainable by between-school factors. In this case, if we omit English Literature, which we have indicated represents an anomalous sample, the range of variation lies between 15 per cent for History and 36 per cent for Maths, with a median of 23 per cent.

Of the proportions of within-school variance accounted for in the regression analyses, represented in column 4, the lowest figure is associated with Spoken English (only eight per cent of occurring variance is explained) and the highest figure with Chemistry (48 per cent of the variance is explained). As proportions of the total variance, the lowest figure is associated with Mathematics, for which only 16 per cent of the total variance is explained by within-school effects, and the other end of the scale is taken by Chemistry, for which 36 per cent is explained (column 6). When we consider the estimates of the proportion of all occurring variance which can be explained by all predictors (column 7), we find that the lowest figure is 36 per cent in the case of Spoken English, and 61 per cent in the case of Chemistry. Although Chemistry, Maths and Physics take the top three places in this column in terms of total explained variance, there does not seem to be a marked subject bias. French features high in the list with a figure of 50 per cent and Biology achieves only 40 per cent. The proportion of within-school variance accounted for (column 4) shows a considerable range; the amount associated with Spoken English (eight per cent) is in sharp contrast with the amounts associated with all other subjects. Once again, Chemistry and Physics take the lead, closely followed by Biology, French and German. The reasons for this pattern may become more apparent when we consider the predictors which contribute to the explanation of variance.

It will be recalled that the variable Attitude is derived from a question probing the feelings of a student when asked about leaving school. We notice that the remarkable thing about Attitude when used as a dependent variable is the small amount of between-school variance (six per cent) associated with it. Apart from this, the profile of Attitude in terms of explained variance is undistinguished and we see in the last column of Table 8.1 that 30 per cent of total variance in Attitude is explained.

We have already referred to the fact that the values of explained variance tend to be over-estimates of the most reliable values. There are two main reasons for this. The first relates to the smaller of the two effects and arises because of the way in which variables are combined after being selected in block-wise fashion. When variables are first selected in blocks, the initial criterion which is applied is that they should contribute significantly (at the five per cent level) to the explanation of variance. Nevertheless, when blocks are combined in the final regression analyses, variables are added to the regression equation which do not contribute significantly in themselves but which collectively tend to inflate the explained variance by a few percentage points. To derive a conservative estimate of explained variance, therefore, the final regression equations have been truncated by inspecting the significance associated with the addition of variables and only those which contribute to prediction at, or beyond, the five per cent significance level have been retained. The figures yielded by this process are listed in Table 8.2 in column 1 headed, 'Raw explained variance between schools.'

The second cause of inflation arises from the small number of degrees of freedom in the regression equations. This particularly affects the between-school analyses, where the degrees of freedom are one less than the number of schools. In this situation, regression tends to capitalize on large correlations leading to an inflated value of explained variance. A correction factor to compensate for this effect is frequently used and is summarized by the following equation:

$$R^2 = 1 - (1 - R^2) \ \frac{N - 1}{N - m - 1}$$

The effect of applying this equation to the figures in column 1 is shown in column 3 of Table 8.2. The within-school variance is affected slightly by the first of these inflating factors and the conservative figures are shown in column 4 where they will be seen to be much the same as the within-school figures quoted in Table 8.1. The new conservative figure of total variance explained is shown in column 5 in Table 8.2, where it can be compared with the uncorrected figure in

Table 8.2: Estimate of explained variance using conservative figures corrected for degrees of freedom: O-level.

Dependent variable	Raw explained variance between schools	Degrees of freedom between schools	Corrected proportion of explained variance			Uncorrected figure	% Reduction required
			of between	of within	total explained		
Biology	.6278	32	.6045	.3073	.3779	.3970	5%
Chemistry	.7684	17	.7275	.4809	.5455	.6127	11%
Maths D	.8152	19	.7763	.2650	.4801	.5207	8%
Physics	.7877	24	.7612	.4078	.5299	.5820	9%
Eng. Lang.	.8880	29	.8610	.2695	.4870	.5078	4%
Eng. Lit. A	.7314	22	.6704	.2901	.3099	.3194	3%
French	.9592	20	.9368	.3167	.4946	.5036	2%
German	.9643	19	.9530	.3100	.4235	.4302	2%
History B	.6894	12	.5600	.2909	.3459	.3845	10%
Geography	.8434	31	.8181	.2967	.4252	.4380	3%
Spoken Eng.	.9398	14	.9097	.0749	.2443	.3593	32%

column 6. We notice, in general, that the correction amounts to between four and 11 per cent over most of the subjects, reaching an extreme in the case of Spoken English where the inflation present in the uncorrected figure amounts to some 30 per cent of that figure. Because the correction is comparatively small in most cases and because it would not in any case affect the block-wise decomposition of variance, it need not be considered further. The corrections included in Table 8.2 imply a harsh consideration of the step-wise regression process and have been included mainly to indicate the magnitude of the effect of correction, which in most cases is comparatively small.

B. *Ordinary level for students with verbal reasoning scores*

We saw in an earlier section that there was evidence that the sample for which verbal reasoning scores were available was not representative of our sample as a whole. In particular, it was evident that the smaller sample was more homogeneous and therefore that the values of omega squared were smaller than for the main sample. Given this situation, it is interesting, quite apart from the influence of the verbal reasoning test on explained variance, to examine to what extent the somewhat different distribution of variance which exists can be explained by the predictors and whether the subject-specific profile is maintained for this reduced sample.

Inspection of column 3 in Table 8.3 indicates that, in common with the main sample analyses, most of the between-school variance which exists is accounted for. Since the between-school variance is itself smaller, however, it follows that if the same proportion of total variance is to be explained in this sample, then the proportion of within-school variance explained by within-school factors must be increased correspondingly. This is found to be the case for each of the dependent variables. For Biology, the proportion of within-school variance explained is increased from 31 to 37 per cent, for English Language from 27 to 36 per cent, for French from 32 to 38 per cent and for Geography from 30 to 33 per cent. The net result of this is not only to maintain the level of total variance explained but to increase it slightly — in general by about four per cent. To some extent, this increase is accounted for by the fact that the sample of schools has been reduced and, therefore, the inflation of explained variance due to reduced degrees of freedom is slightly greater in the case of this analysis than in the main analysis. In principle, it could be that the addition of a new block, namely 'Verbal Reasoning Test' which also includes age,

Table 8.3: Composition of explained variance for samples with verbal reasoning scores: O-level.

Dependent variable	ω²	Within as proportion of total	Explained between	Explained within	Explained between of total	Explained within of total	Explained of total
Biology	.1686	.8314	.9851	.3694	.1661	.3071	.4732
Eng. Lang.	.3458	.6542	.9941	.3565	.3438	.2332	.5770
French	.1497	.8502	.9758	.3804	.1461	.3234	.4695
Geography	.2502	.7498	.9693	.3326	.2425	.2494	.4919

Table 8.4: Composition of explained variance: A-level.

Dependent variable	ω²	Estimated proportion of within	Between variance explained	Within variance explained	Between explained of total	Within explained of total	Proportion of total explained	Conservative estimate
Maths	.1264	.8735	.9684	.4966	.1225	.4338	.5563	.5454
Eng. Lit.	.2237	.7763	.9914	.3013	.2218	.2339	.4557	.4083
French	.2024	.7976	.9444	.4238	.1911	.3380	.5292	.5096
Geography	.3248	.6752	.9999	.2442	.3248	.1649	.4897	.4488
Attitude	.1445	.8555	.9491	.0633	.1371	.0541	.1913	.1748

could inflate the variance explained but we shall see when we come to examine the breakdown of explained variance in more detail that this is not sufficient to account for the difference detected.

C. Advanced level examinations

The proportions of variance explained for A-level examinations are shown in Table 8.4. Here we notice that the values of omega squared differ from those applied to examinations with similar subject names at O-level. We must, of course, discount English Literature from this comparison because of the anomalous sample at the O-level, but in the case of Mathematics we see that omega squared at A-level is very much smaller, while that for Geography is somewhat larger than at O-level. Once again, of the variation which exists, we find (column 3) that most of it is explained by the predictors. The range of values representing within-school variance explained in column 4 is not remarkable in its difference from O-level, with the exception of Attitude, where the proportion of variance explained has gone down from 26 per cent in the case of O-level to six per cent in the case of A-level. This is reflected in the proportion of total variance explained for Attitude, where the figure is now only 19 per cent compared with 30 per cent for O-level. The inference here is that the student's attitude to staying at school is much less open to prediction at A-level than was the case at O-level. We shall have a clearer idea of the structure of this phenomenon when we come to examine the pattern of predictors at A-level. In general, with the exception of Attitude, we see that the proportion of total explained variance at A-level is similar to, but slightly greater than, that explained at O-level.

Column 8 of Table 8.4 presents the conservative estimate of explained variance derived in exactly the same way as that described in connection with Table 8.2 and here we notice that the order of magnitude of the discrepancy is similar to that arising in connection with O-level examinations.

Decomposition of variance

The next stage in examining the variance which can be explained by the regression analyses is to assess the contributions to explanation by individual blocks. We shall assess the contribution of each block to the total explained variance in terms of its unique contribution and its contribution in common with all other blocks included in that section of the regression analysis. This will be done for all subjects at O-level

Table 8.5: Percentages of total variance in dependent variables explained uniquely and in common by each block of predictors: O-level.

Dependent variable		Between school						Within school				
		Teacher	School	Parent Body	Student Body	School-Individual	Total explained between	Family	Individual	Conformity to Press	Total explained within	Total explained variance
Biology	unique	0.1	0.1	1.1	0.3	0.9		0.0	19.3	0.0		
	shared	5.2	12.4	11.2	10.4	9.3		2.4	3.7	2.3		
	TOTAL	5.3	12.5	12.3	10.7	10.2	15.9	2.4	23.0	2.3	23.8	39.7
Chemistry	unique	2.9	3.4	0.3	0.1	0.9		0.0	32.6	0.0		
	shared	8.9	3.1	16.8	3.7	10.6		1.0	3.0	2.1		
	TOTAL	11.8	6.5	17.1	3.8	11.5	25.7	1.0	35.6	2.1	35.6	61.3
Maths D	unique	1.0	8.1	0.7	0.7	0.0		0.0	12.8	0.0		
	shared	16.8	25.7	5.0	7.0	12.3		1.9	2.2	1.0		
	TOTAL	17.8	33.8	5.7	7.7	12.3	36.3	1.9	15.0	1.0	15.8	52.1
Physics	unique	1.8	2.6	1.2	1.3	1.0		0.0	25.4	0.0		
	shared	10.0	23.3	18.2	13.8	13.6		1.3	2.0	1.0		
	TOTAL	11.8	25.9	19.4	15.1	14.6	30.6	1.3	27.4	1.0	27.6	58.2
Eng. Lang.	unique	0.4	2.7	0.5	0.3	0.5		0.0	13.5	0.0		
	shared	10.0	7.7	17.0	19.5	28.4		1.9	3.2	2.3		
	TOTAL	10.4	10.4	17.5	18.8	28.9	33.4	1.9	16.7	2.3	17.4	50.8
Eng. Lit A	unique	0.2	0.4	0.0	0.0	0.5		0.0	22.9	0.3		
	shared	1.7	2.5	0.9	0.9	2.4		2.3	4.6	2.6		
	TOTAL	1.9	2.9	0.9	0.9	2.9	4.0	2.3	27.5	2.9	27.9	31.9

Table 8.5: Percentages of total variance in dependent variables explained uniquely and in common by each block of predictors: O-level. *Continued*

French	unique	5.0	1.4	1.9	2.3	2.3		0.0	20.6	0.1		
	shared	11.8	17.1	13.3	9.2	14.8		1.7	2.4	0.9		
	TOTAL	16.8	18.5	15.2	11.5	17.1	27.2	1.7	23.0	1.0	23.1	50.4
German	unique	5.3	0.2	0.6	0.4	1.1		0.0	21.9	0.2		
	shared	9.5	10.4	5.1	4.3	1.8		2.4	3.7	1.4		
	TOTAL	14.8	10.6	5.7	4.7	2.9	17.2	2.4	25.6	1.6	25.8	43.0
History	unique	0.0	4.6	0.6	0.1	0.1		0.1	18.9	0.5		
	shared	0.0	8.8	3.5	4.9	7.2		3.2	4.3	1.5		
	TOTAL	0.0	13.4	4.1	5.0	7.3	14.6	3.3	23.2	2.0	23.8	38.5
Geography	unique	1.0	4.1	0.2	0.0	0.2		0.1	18.7	0.0		
	shared	4.5	15.3	7.7	8.4	15.5		2.4	3.8	1.7		
	TOTAL	5.5	19.4	7.9	8.4	15.7	21.1	2.5	22.5	1.7	22.7	43.8
Spoken Eng.	unique	1.8	0.4	0.2	0.3	1.0		0.4	4.4	0.4		
	shared	14.5	13.9	5.3	12.6	15.1		0.6	1.0	0.4		
	TOTAL	16.3	14.3	5.5	12.9	16.1	19.7	1.0	5.4	0.8	16.2	35.9
Attitude	unique	—	1.1	0.2	1.0	0.3		0.3	13.6	0.0		
	shared	—	3.2	1.7	3.1	2.1		2.4	6.4	7.8		
	TOTAL	—	4.3	1.9	4.1	2.4	6.2	2.7	20.0	7.8	23.9	30.1

and A-level and for the sample for whom verbal reasoning test scores
were available.

A. Ordinary level examinations

Total variance

Data for the Ordinary level examinations are presented in Table 8.5,
where the variance explained by between-school effects and that
explained by within-school effects are decomposed separately. In the
first row for each subject variable, we present the unique contribution
of each block as a percentage of total variance which exists and in the
second row we present the percentage of variance explained by each
block in common with all others in that group. For example, in the case
of Biology, the Teacher block makes virtually no unique contribution
to the variance, but in combination with School, Parent Body, Student
Body and School–Individual blocks, it accounts for 5.2 per cent of
total criterion variance. It should be noted that there can be no
commonality between any of these five blocks and the Family,
Individual and Conformity to Press blocks, since the five blocks belong
to between-school and the other three blocks to within-school parts of
the analysis. The figures in this table are rounded up to the first decimal
place which means that in some cases the totals recorded are not the
precise sum of individual items in the table.

The within-school and between-school analyses present entirely
different pictures. The first thing that emerges from a consideration of
the within-school analysis is that not only is the Individual block the
highest contributor to explained variance, but much of this contribution is unique to that block. By contrast the unique contribution of
the Family block to explanation of variance is virtually zero for all
variables. In the case of Spoken English, it is interesting to note that the
variance which can be explained by within-school factors collectively is
smaller than for all other dependent variables.

Explained variance

Table 8.6 sets out the data in a way which enables us to assess the
relative contribution of individual blocks to explained variance. The
discussion for this table begins with column 1 where the total variance
explained by all predictors is set out for each of the dependent
variables. In the case of Biology, this figure is 39.7 per cent. Of the
variance explained, the Teacher and School blocks each contribute 0.3

Table 8.6: Percentages of explained variance in dependent variables contributed by blocks of predictors: O-level.

Dependent variable	Total explained variance	Between school Unique contributions						Within school Unique contributions			
		Teacher	School	Parent Body	Student Body	School-Individual	Commonality	Family	Individual	Conformity to Press	Commonality
Biology	39.7	0.3	0.3	2.8	0.8	2.3	33.6	0.0	48.6	0.0	11.3
Chemistry	61.2	4.8	5.5	0.4	0.2	1.5	29.5	0.0	53.3	0.0	4.9
Maths D	52.1	1.8	15.6	1.4	1.3	0.0	49.5	0.0	24.6	0.0	5.7
Physics	58.2	3.2	4.5	2.1	2.2	1.8	38.8	0.0	43.6	0.0	3.8
Eng. Lang.	50.8	0.7	5.3	1.0	0.6	1.1	57.1	0.0	26.6	0.0	7.7
Eng. Lit. A	31.9	0.6	1.3	0.1	0.0	1.6	9.0	0.0	71.7	0.9	14.9
French	50.4	9.9	2.9	3.8	4.5	4.6	28.4	0.0	40.9	0.2	4.7
German	43.0	12.4	0.5	1.3	1.0	2.5	22.3	0.0	50.9	0.5	8.6
History	38.5	0.0	12.1	1.5	0.3	0.2	23.9	0.3	49.1	1.3	11.1
Geography	43.8	2.3	9.3	0.4	0.0	0.4	35.8	0.2	42.6	0.0	9.0
Spoken Eng.	35.9	5.0	1.2	0.5	0.8	2.8	44.7	1.5	12.3	1.5	29.8
Attitude	30.1	—	3.7	0.7	3.3	1.0	12.0	1.0	45.2	0.0	33.2

Table 8.7: Percentages of explained between-school variance in dependent variables contributed by each of the blocks of variables composed of school means: O-level.

Dependent variable		Between variance explained	Teacher	School	Parent Body	Student Body	School-Individual	Commonality	Between as percentage of total
					Unique contributions				
Biology	Unique	67.0	0.8	0.8	6.9	2.0	5.7	50.8	15.9
	total		33.0	78.5	77.2	67.2	64.3		
Chemistry	Unique	98.52	11.4	13.1	1.1	0.4	3.7	68.8	25.7
	total		45.8	25.4	66.5	15.0	44.7		
Maths D	Unique	86.2	2.6	22.4	2.1	1.8	0.1	57.2	36.3
	total		93.3	49.2	15.7	21.2	34.0		
Physics	Unique	98.4	6.0	8.5	4.0	4.1	3.4	65.3	30.6
	total		38.4	84.7	63.4	49.3	47.5		
Eng. Lang.	Unique	98.6	1.1	8.0	1.6	0.9	1.6	77.7	33.4
	total		37.3	91.6	52.4	59.2	86.6		
Eng. Lit. A	Unique	91.8	4.5	10.5	0.8	0.4	12.4	49.7	4.0
	total		47.0	72.0	4.5	23.3	71.6		
French	Unique	98.5	18.3	5.3	7.0	8.3	8.5	48.7	27.2
	total		61.6	67.8	55.9	42.1	62.8		
German	Unique	96.2	30.9	1.2	3.4	2.5	6.2	53.5	17.2
	total		86.0	61.5	32.9	27.2	16.9		
History B	Unique	98.1	—	31.7	4.1	0.8	0.5	34.8	14.6
	total		—	91.4	27.9	33.9	49.9		

Table 8.7: Percentages of explained between-school variance in dependent variables contributed by each of the blocks of variables composed of school means: O-level. *continued.*

Geography	Unique	89.6	4.8	19.3	0.8	0.0	0.7	21.1
	total		26.1	91.8	37.5	39.8	74.3	60.2
Spoken Eng	Unique	99.7	9.0	2.2	0.8	1.5	5.1	19.7
	total		82.3	72.5	27.8	65.1	81.5	78.7
Attitude	Unique	71.4		17.6	2.8	16.7	4.0	6.2
	total			48.7	22.0	47.5	26.6	42.4

Table 8.8: Overlap between pairs of blocks as percentages of explained between-school variance: O-level.

Dependent variable	Teacher/ School	Teacher/ Parent Body	Teacher/ Student Body	Teacher/ School– Individual	School/ Parent Body	School/ Student Body	School/ School– Individual	Parent body/ Student Body	Parent body/ School– Individual	Student body/ School– Individual
Biology	1.1	−0.1	0.0	0.8	7.1	0.0	5.4	4.7	−2.3	4.2
Chemistry	−5.3	2.4	2.4	4.3	6.0	1.9	7.0	4.8	2.1	7.2
Maths D	19.6	0.6	0.6	0.0	−2.0	6.1	23.1	−0.5	0.3	0.0
Physics	2.6	3.9	1.8	4.0	15.6	4.1	2.8	−3.1	0.0	0.3
Eng. Lang.	0.2	−0.4	−0.5	0.5	−0.3	1.9	6.5	−0.5	2.7	1.9
Eng. Lit.	5.2	0.1	0.4	2.5	0.8	−0.4	10.3	0.4	−0.8	13.0
French	−2.7	−4.9	−4.9	−4.1	−4.7	−2.7	−3.8	−0.9	−3.0	4.3
German	22.8	3.0	−0.8	−1.7	1.1	0.4	0.6	−2.7	−2.2	4.4
History	—	—	—	—	2.6	15.4	16.3	0.6	3.0	−0.1
Geography	−3.2	−0.6	0.4	1.3	−0.7	4.2	28.6	0.1	−0.3	0.6
Spoken Eng.	2.2	1.5	−1.3	2.1	0.7	2.4	0.3	−0.8	−0.8	1.8

per cent, the Parent Body 2.8 per cent and so on with 33.6 per cent of the explained variance being contributed by the commonality of all five blocks in the between-school analysis. Of the remaining variance required to make up 100 per cent, we see on the right of the table that 48.6 per cent is contributed uniquely by the Individual block and 11.3 per cent by the commonality between the three blocks of the within-school analysis. The generally low unique contributions of variance by most of the blocks may be noted, contrasting with the Individual block which contributes amounts ranging from 12.3 per cent in the case of Spoken English to 53.3 per cent for Chemistry.

Because the between-school variance explained is a relatively small proportion of the total explained variance, it could be that Table 8.6 is concealing contributions to between-school variance as a result of rounding errors. To overcome this difficulty we present in Table 8.7 a breakdown of the unique contributions of blocks to the explanation of between-school variance alone. Column 1 presents the percentage of between-school variance that is explained and, as we have already seen, this is close to 100 per cent in the case of most of the dependent variables. The reader should note that the second line of each subject variable shows the figure for the total contribution to between-school variance by each block, despite the confusing reference to 'unique contributions' at the head of the columns.

Table 8.8 contains commonalities between blocks in the between-school analysis. The figures in the table are obtained by summing the percentage of explained variance with which each pair of blocks is jointly associated. The data in the table enable us to examine the hypothesis that particular pairs of blocks may display much higher commonality than other pairs. A perusal of the data demonstrates that this is not the case; it can be seen that the overlap is distributed throughout the between-school blocks and appears not to be subject-specific in any way which is clearly discernible.

B. Ordinary level for students with verbal reasoning scores

Because of the way in which the verbal reasoning variable was entered into the analysis, there is a significant change in the block structure in this instance. In the case of the school mean blocks, the new block containing verbal reasoning test score and age replaces the Parent Body block. This new block also contains school means and the two variables within it signify the mean performance of pupils on a verbal reasoning test taken at the time they entered secondary school and the mean age of students, also at time of entry. This block is labelled Entry Characteristics.

In the within-school blocks, the new block is an addition and is called Entry Characteristics. It contains the deviation scores of the pupils on a verbal reasoning test at entry to the school and their age at that time. In calculating age, it is assumed that the age of a student at entry will differ from his current age by a fixed number of years. This would usually be the case but may not be so for a minority of pupils who are retaking their O-level examination or have repeated a class during their school careers.

We have already remarked that the sample involved in the verbal reasoning test analysis differs from that used in the main analysis and that the between-school analyses are not comparable; a glance at Tables 8.9 and 8.5 indicate that there are obvious differences between the tables in the extent to which variance is explained and in how blocks contribute to the explanation. In neither the between-school nor within-school analyses, does the addition of verbal reasoning score/age (described as Entry Mean in the former and Entry Characteristic in the latter) offer much unique contribution to the explanation of variance.

C. Advanced level examinations

Table 8.10 displays the breakdown of variance in the case of Advanced level subjects and, in the information it displays, it is similar to Table 8.5. Table 8.11 shows the contribution of different blocks in terms of their unique and shared components as percentages of the total variance explained. This table is comparable to Table 8.6 for the O-level results. Again we see the predominant source of variation is the Individual block. For all four examination subjects, it contributes more to the unique explanation of variance than any other block (ranging from 30 to 66 per cent). Its contribution in the case of Attitude is small (11.5 per cent) in comparison with its contribution to examination variance. For Attitude, the largest unique contribution comes from the Conformity to Press block (13.1 per cent). Attitude, in fact, is poorly predicted by other variables in the Individual block at the A-level and the little variance that can be predicted arises through the common-alities of a number of blocks. This is in sharp contrast to the O-level, where Attitude is uniquely predicted by the Individual block with a value of 45.2 per cent, and the contribution of the Individual block in common with other blocks is 78.4 per cent. The pattern seems to be one in which the aspirations and expectations of the individual, which

Table 8.9: Percentages of total variance in dependent variables explained uniquely and in common by each of the blocks of predictors when verbal reasoning and age are included: O-level.

Dependent variable		Family	Individual	Conformity to Press	Entry characteristics	Total explained within	Total explained variance
Biology	unique	1.4	21.5	0.7	0.7		
	common	3.3	6.3	2.4	1.7		
	TOTAL	4.7	27.8	3.1	2.4	30.7	47.3
Eng. Lang.	unique	0.0	12.5	0.2	2.4		
	common	1.8	8.2	1.6	6.5		
	TOTAL	1.8	20.7	1.8	8.9	23.3	57.7
French	unique	0.4	27.4	0.0	0.9		
	common	1.2	3.7	1.0	2.3		
	TOTAL	1.6	31.1	1.0	3.2	32.3	47.0
Geography	unique	0.4	19.5	0.3	0.3		
	common	2.8	4.4	0.6	1.9		
	TOTAL	3.2	23.9	0.9	2.2	24.9	49.2

Table 8.10: Percentages of total variance in dependent variables explained uniquely and in common by each block of predictors: A-level.

Dependent variable		Between school						Within school				
		Teacher	School	Parent Body	Student Body	School–Individual	Total explained between	Family	Individual	Conformity to Press	Total explained within	Total explained variance
Pure Maths	unique	0.3	0.1	0.2	2.1	0.1		0.0	36.7	0.0		
	common	4.4	7.2	5.2	9.1	5.9		1.6	6.2	5.9		
	Total	4.7	7.3	5.4	11.2	6.0	12.2	1.6	42.9	5.9	43.4	55.6
Eng. Lit.	unique	0.9	0.5	1.1	1.6	0.4		0.0	20.9	1.0		
	common	10.1	12.4	8.6	10.9	6.7		0.0	1.2	1.0		
	Total	11.0	12.9	9.7	12.5	7.1	22.1	0.0	22.1	2.1	23.4	45.5
French	unique	2.6	-1.0	0.0	0.0	-0.7		1.2	27.9	1.7		
	common	13.2	14.5	1.6	11.8	6.0		1.6	3.3	0.7		
	Total	15.8	13.5	1.6	11.8	5.3	19.1	2.8	31.2	2.4	33.8	52.9
Geography	unique	0.5	0.4	0.4	2.5	1.0		0.0	14.6	0.0		
	common	19.6	30.3	15.5	14.5	26.5		1.3	1.3	0.0		
	Total	20.1	30.7	15.9	17.0	27.5	32.4	1.3	15.9	0.0	16.5	48.9
Attitude	unique	—	2.0	0.5	0.2	1.2		0.0	2.2	2.5		
	common	—	8.7	0.9	6.1	7.3		0.0	0.5	0.6		
	Total	—	10.7	1.4	6.3	8.5	13.7	0.0	2.7	3.1	5.4	19.1

Table 8.11: Percentages of explained variance in dependent variables contributed by blocks of predictors: A-level.

Dependent variable	Total explained variance	Between school Unique contributions						Within school Unique contributions			
		Teacher	School	Parent Body	Student Body	School–Individual	Common-ality	Family	Individual	Conformity to Press	Commonality
Pure Maths	55.6	0.5	0.2	0.4	3.8	0.2	16.9	0.0	66.0	0.0	12.1
Eng. Lit	45.5	2.0	1.1	2.4	3.5	0.2	38.7	0.0	45.9	2.2	3.3
French	52.9	4.9	-1.9	0.0	0.0	-1.3	34.4	2.3	52.7	3.2	5.7
Geography	48.9	1.0	0.8	0.8	5.1	2.0	56.4	0.0	29.9	0.0	4.3
Attitude	19.1		10.5	2.6	1.0	6.3	51.3	0.0	11.5	13.1	3.7

mainly comprise the Individual block, have a decreasing influence over the variable Attitude, which is the student's desire to stay at school. This is perhaps to be expected in a survey carried out during the student's final year in school.

Before turning attention to the between-school effects, it will be useful to examine Table 8.12, which like Table 8.7 for the O-level examinations, displays the contribution to variance as a percentage of explained between-school variance. In the case of Pure Maths, of the variance which exists between schools, 17.4 per cent is accounted for by the Student Body block uniquely. This contrasts very sharply with the O-level results for Mathematics in which, although the Student Body block in common with other blocks explains 70 per cent of the between-school variance, none of this is unique to that block. Geography presents a distribution rather similar to that found for Mathematics, while in the case of English Literature, we find less unique prediction. In the case of French, 13.5 per cent of variance is uniquely explained by the Teacher block, with virtually no contribution from the remaining blocks.

In view of the relatively large commonality existing in the between-school analyses, it may be of interest to examine the degree of overlap that occurs between pairs of blocks. This information is presented in Table 8.13, where every pair of the five between-school blocks is presented. No very salient pattern emerges, but the case of French is interesting since there appear to be minimal overlaps between the Parent Body block and each of the other four blocks. This is clearly due to the fact that Parent Body contributes very little toward explanation of variance in French, as a glance at Table 8.10 will show. The remaining patterns which occur are largely attributable to the variance explained in total by different blocks and we must conclude that the linkage displayed in this table does not warrant any hypotheses of structural association.

Conclusion

The first thing we may note for the O-level examination is that the amount of variance that is explained in the regression analyses ranges from 32 per cent in the case of English Literature to 61 per cent in the case of Chemistry (Table 8.1). For the majority of subjects, approximately half the total variance is explained. In the two cases where it is low, English Literature and Spoken English, the subjectivity of marking is likely to have seriously affected reliability of marks.

Table 8.12: Percentages of explained between-school variance in dependent variables contributed by each of the blocks of variables composed of school means: A-level.

Dependent variable	Between variance explained	Unique contributions					Commonality	Between as percentage of total
		Teacher	School	Parent Body	Student Body	School—Individual		
Pure Maths	96.8	2.1	1.1	1.8	17.4	1.0	76.4	12.2
Eng. Lit.	99.1	4.0	2.2	4.8	7.3	1.7	79.1	22.1
French	94.4	13.5	−5.4	0.0	0.1	−3.8	90.0	19.1
Geography	99.9	1.5	1.1	1.3	7.9	3.0	85.1	32.4
Attitude	94.9	—	14.9	3.4	1.3	9.0	66.3	13.7

Table 8.13: Overlap between pairs of blocks as percentages of explained between-school variance: A-level.

Dependent variable	Teacher/ School	Teacher/ Parent Body	Teacher/ Student Body	Teacher/ School– Individual	School/ Parent Body	School/ Student Body	School/ School– Individual	Parent Body/ Student Body	Parent Body/ School– Individual	Student Body/ School– Individual
Pure Maths	27.3	12.7	35.6	11.5	30.5	57.0	44.8	43.3	28.1	45.9
Eng. Lit.	38.4	14.3	19.9	13.1	34.4	27.8	22.2	37.0	19.0	24.8
French	69.2	8.5	44.6	19.7	6.6	49.4	25.5	8.3	1.1	20.0
Geography	61.7	42.9	24.3	57.4	48.8	50.5	82.0	34.8	41.4	44.9
Attitude	—	—	—	—	9.1	38.7	31.1	8.7	3.4	23.6

Of the variance that occurs, for all subjects, the greater proportion is within rather than between schools. It ranges from a low of 57.9 per cent in the case of Mathematics to a high of 94.9 per cent in the case of English Literature. At the same time, the proportion of total variance that exists between schools is not inconsequential. With the exception of English Literature, which at 5.2 per cent is exceptionally low, the proportion of total variance that lies between schools ranges from a low of 20.3 per cent for History and Spoken English to a high of 42.1 per cent for Mathematics (Table 8.1).

Most of the between-school variance, as expected, is explained in our regression analyses. The amount ranges between 67 and 99 per cent. On the other hand, less than half the within-school variance is explained. The amount explained was lowest in the case of Spoken English (eight per cent), and highest in the case of Chemistry (48 per cent) (Table 8.1).

It was possible to include verbal reasoning test scores as regressor variables only in the case of four dependent variables. The effect of including these scores was to increase slightly the total amount of variance explained in the dependent measures; furthermore, the proportion of within-school relative to between-school variance increased somewhat. Overall, however, the inclusion of the verbal reasoning scores did not substantially alter the results of the full-sample analysis. In any case, the different treatment of the regression equations and the inclusion of additional variables make any comparison suspect.

When we look at the contribution of blocks to the explanation of between-school variance, we find that in the case of only one subject (Mathematics) is there a unique contribution of more than eight per cent by any block (Table 8.5). It is clear that it is the concerted function of blocks, rather than the unique contributions of individual blocks, that enables achievement to be explained. All blocks contribute substantially. In only one subject, Chemistry, does the Family block have the largest shared contribution. For seven of the 11 subjects, it is the School or Teacher block that makes the largest contribution and for the remaining three it is the block representing School—Individual.

In the explanation of within-school variance, the situation is quite different. Here, the Individual block, in every case, makes a unique contribution which is the greater part of explained variance.

The results for A-level subjects are in general similar to those obtained for O-level subjects. In the case of the former, there was a tendency for the proportion of variance explained to be slightly larger than that explained at O-level.

Finally, we may say a word about the single non-cognitive variable included as a dependent variable in our analyses. Practically all variance (91 per cent) in this measure was within rather than between schools. Otherwise, the measure behaved in a fashion rather similar to the cognitive measures.

Chapter Nine

Interpretation of Between-School Regression Analyses

In this chapter we offer an interpretation of the regression analyses that led to the partitioning of variance in examination achievement considered in the last chapter. Such an interpretation is necessary because of the changing character of the blocks as the analysis proceeds and as attrition of variables leaves others to carry the representation of the original corpus. After an exploration of the effects of selective and Maintained/non-Maintained school factors, each O-level subject will be discussed.

In considering the results of the regression analyses, it is important to bear in mind the influence of the self-selective nature of the samples upon the variation in achievement between schools for each subject. The chapter on sampling has already drawn attention to the sex bias in the sample and to the preponderance of candidates from selective schools. Perhaps the most important feature to attend to is the extent to which the between-school variance is a function of differences between selective and non-selective schools. In Table 9.1, the performances of candidates from Independent, Direct Grant and Grammar schools are contrasted with the performances of those from Secondary Modern, Comprehensive and other secondary schools. While in both Independent and Direct Grant schools there is a selective feature arising from the payment of fees which is directly related to social class, all those in Grammar schools and a substantial proportion of those in Direct Grant schools would not be fee-paying but would have been selected with reference to their academic aptitude at age eleven. The

Table 9.1: Proportions of between-school variance associated with difference between selective and non-selective schools: O-level examinations.

Dependent variable	Total sample				Selective schools			Non-selective schools				Between selective and non-selective schools	
	$\bar{X}$	N	M	MSB	$\bar{X}$	N	M	$\bar{X}$	N	M	MSB	MSB	$\%$
Biology	49.47	1062	35	1828.02	52.10	691	16	44.42	371	19	26,123.72	42.0
Chemistry	53.73	461	21	2263.20	60.63	333	10	47.22	128	11	11,913.30	26.3
Maths. D	47.08	618	24	4826.00	50.19	400	11	47.08	218	13	10,984.00	9.9
Physics	52.36	550	28	1942.24	55.77	388	12	44.22	162	16	15,244.29	29.1
Eng. Lang.	53.73	1929	37	3047.31	60.63	937	15	47.22	992	23	86,757.19	79.1
Eng. Lit.	47.34	1064	28	524.41	47.69	578	12	46.92	486	16	157.73	1.1
French	61.13	1351	32	3172.50	63.61	843	16	57.03	508	16	13,714.62	13.9
German	51.35	494	26	957.41	56.34	299	15	43.70	195	11	18,852.35	78.8
Geography	46.55	1208	37	1751.49	49.79	672	16	42.48	536	20	15,964.81	25.3
History B	45.99	648	18	1260.89	47.50	468	13	42.08	180	5	3,808.21	17.8
Spoken Eng.	63.12	1165	22	1837.46	65.77	767	13	58.98	398	9	12,220.82	31.7

table displays the means for the total sample in each subject and for each of these subgroups of candidates from selective and non-selective schools. It also displays the mean square between selective and non-selective schools and gives the percentage of between-school variance which the selective/non-selective factor accounts for. The very large differences in the proportion accounted for emphasizes the diversity of the selective contribution. Interpretation of the contribution of the blocks of variables to the explanation of between-school variance must take such differences into account.

The extent of the effect of the selective factor upon potential candidacy and subsequent success in O-levels is perhaps best demonstrated by English Language which with 1,292 candidates and 37 schools has by far the largest candidacy of any subject. There is less pre-selection in English Language than in the case of other subjects. It is the only subject in which a higher proportion of candidates comes from non-selective schools. Only Mathematics has a higher proportion of variance which lies between schools; yet of the English Language between-school variance, almost 80 per cent is accounted for by the selective—non-selective factor. Thus, the most complete estimate we have of differences between schools, rather than of subject-specific samples from schools, is that the greater part of the variation arises from differences in academic aptitude and social class which had determined school admission. The high total contribution of School (91.6 per cent) and School—Individual (86.6 per cent) blocks to between-school variance supports this interpretation. In the following subject by subject interpretation of the between-schools regression analysis, we shall keep this selective admission effect in focus. Unless otherwise stated, the variances of which proportions are given are explained between-school variances, which for O-level results can be found in Table 8.7 and for A-level results can be derived from Table 8.12. Tables 9.2 to 9.16 list the variables entering the final regression analyses for each subject and their step-wise effect on prediction. The key to the acronyms for each variable and the directional sense of each variable's measurement can be found in Chapter Six.

A. Ordinary level examinations

Biology

Biology is unusual in the low amount of between-school variance that is explained by the regression analyses (67 per cent). While this subject shows a substantial selective admission effect, with 42 per cent of between-school variance accounted for, the social class effect associated with non-Maintained schools is not so strong. Twenty-nine per cent of between-school variance is accounted for by the difference between non-Maintained and Maintained schools. It is thus not surprising to find the high negative correlation with Maintained schools in the analyses of the School block variables. Similarly, the teachers in the higher scoring schools express the view that study is important to all pupils, a view more likely to be held in selective non-Maintained schools. Thus, schools are being defined less in terms of their facilities than in terms of their organizational character which reflects their association with selective admission.

The variables surviving in the Teacher block are interesting. While one might have expected to see some emphasis on practical work, the only teaching technique positively associated with achievement is discussion. Writing is negatively correlated. In the Student Body block, there is a positive correlation with time spent in studying which is unusually high (.63) and a negative correlation with age which is also greater than expected (.49). There are no surprises in the Parent Body block, social class being positively correlated with achievement and help given by the home being negatively correlated. The School—Individual block confirms that higher achievement is associated with the pupils perceiving the school as making study important for all pupils and as being intolerant of the less academic.

Table 9.2: Between-school final regression analysis: Biology O-level.

Variable	Simple r	Standardized B	R^2
FAJOB	−.68	−.44	.46
OPIN1	−.64	−.33	.63
TOPIN1	−.69	−.11	.65
TMSTUDY	.63	.12	.66
DISCUSS	.37	−.10	.66
AGE	−.49	−.09	.67
HMHELP	−.36	−.05	.67
WRITE	−.35	−.03	.67
SOPIN5	.42	−.02	.67
MAINTAIN	−.63	.01	.67

Table 9.3: **Between-school final regression analysis: Mathematics (D) O-level.**

Variable	Simple r	Standardized B	R^2
PUPIL16	.71	.46	.50
LABS	.49	.42	.68
STR2	−.49	−.33	.77
LECTURE	−.61	−.16	.82
STR1	.02	−.14	.83
FAJOB	−.37	.18	.84
ATTITUDE	.43	.17	.85
TRAIN	.31	.13	.86
SOPIN3	.54	.04	.86

Mathematics (D)

For Mathematics, whereas a high proportion (86 per cent) of the between-school variance is accounted for by the independent variables, less than ten per cent of the between-school variance is explained by differences between selective and non-selective schools. Thus, one would expect to find, in the case of this subject, evidence of other than a collusive effect. The largest total contribution comes from the Teacher block but there is a high unique contribution from the School block. Of the variables surviving in the School block, that indicating the number of pupils aged 16 and over makes the largest contribution to explained variance. It appears that this indicates the size of sixth forms which would also be a measure of the number and possible level of posts held by specialized teachers. Another substantial contribution indicates the practice of homogeneous ability grouping in higher scoring schools. The positive correlation of the number of laboratories in schools with achievement is possibly an indirect indication of the emphasis in such schools on Mathematics in association with science subjects, and of separate provision for sixth form students.

The Teacher block contains only two variables, one indicating training in the teaching of Mathematics and the other, avoidance of lecture techniques, presumably in favour of the working of examples. The single surviving School—Individual variable denies a stress on good habits and self-expression and by implication greater emphasis on academic conformity. The Student Body block also contains only one variable, which is positively related to achievement − the desire to continue study in school. The lack of a strong social class influence is confirmed by the low correlation of father's job, the only surviving family variable, with achievement in Mathematics.

The overall interpretation that arises from the results in Mathematics reinforces the view that higher achieving schools are those which

Table 9.4: Between-school final regression analysis: Chemistry O-level.

Variable	Simple r	Standardized B	R^2
FAJOB	−.71	−.22	.50
LECTURE	.60	.29	.70
OPIN3	.49	.44	.77
ATTITUDE	.34	−.11	.80
HMHELP	−.19	−.37	.84
SSEXF	−.11	−.42	.90
PRACT	.21	.73	.93
ADMISS1	.49	.50	.98
SOPIN6	.42	−.08	.99

Table 9.5: Between-school final regression analysis: Physics O-level.

Variable	Simple r	Standardized B	R^2
MAINTAIN	−.76	−.16	.58
PRACT	.58	.46	.73
ADMISS1	.47	−.18	.79
ADMISS3	−.66	−.15	.82
OPIN3	.57	−.21	.84
OPIN1	−.52	.13	.85
DISCUSS	.20	.73	.87
ATTITUDE	.52	.04	.87
HMHELP	−.07	−.73	.87
TMSTUDY	.51	.31	.88
SOPIN3	.43	.24	.89
FRSPACE	−.33	.45	.89
FAJOB	−.72	−.52	.91

maximize the interaction between ability of pupils in Mathematics and expert teaching. The effect is in this case not one dependent upon prior selection of the intake so much as a bringing together of school based and student resources towards maximum achievement output.

Chemistry and Physics

It is a reasonable contention that those subjects which are most likely to respond to the examination of school effects are those which rely most heavily upon specialized instruction (Lindquist, 1966). Mathematics and the natural sciences should, on this argument, be susceptible to the demonstration of school-based effects. We have already examined Mathematics and found support. We may look at Chemistry and Physics in the same way. Both subjects show that over a quarter of the between-school variance is associated with selective admission effect. In both subjects too, the proportion of between variance contributed by Maintained/non-Maintained school division is about the same, 32.11 per cent for Physics and 29.08 per cent for Chemistry. In both subjects, the Teacher and School blocks make the largest unique contribution to the explanation of between-school variance.

Here the resemblance ends since, while the proportion of variance contributed by the Parent Body blocks in concert with others is almost the same (Chemistry 65 per cent, Physics 59 per cent), in the case of Physics, the concerted effect of the School block is much larger (Chemistry 12 per cent, Physics 76 per cent). In other words, if the Parent Body block were removed from the partitioning for each subject, 32 to 35 per cent of variance would be explicable by the other blocks, but if the School block were removed, in the case of Chemistry 73 per cent would remain, while in the case of Physics only 14 per cent would remain.

Examination of the variables surviving into the regression analysis from the School block confirms the similarity between subjects in the composition of the sample. Both show a positive simple correlation for Admission factor 1 with achievement, a factor which relates to the use of examinations and primary school reports in selection procedures and indicates higher performance as being associated with use of examinations for selection. Factor 1 is characteristic of Direct Grant and Independent schools. Chemistry additionally shows discrimination against school sex being female. For both subjects, higher achievement is associated with a preference for staying on at school and with time spent in private study. The social class of father's job is positively related and help given by the home is negatively related for both subjects. The teacher variables indicate the positive contribution of practical work, more so in Physics than in Chemistry, and the opinion of students in higher achieving schools is that, for both subjects, examination performance is more important than study for its own sake.

Differences between the subjects are apparent in the teaching techniques, lecture methods making a positive contribution for Chemistry and discussion for Physics. Differences between the higher scoring schools in each subject are also evident; amongst those in Physics, study is seen as important to all pupils and good behaviour is stressed, whereas for those in Chemistry it is hard work. It seems that these subjects behave as expected, in being responsive to school effects in similar ways, although Physics shows more signs of being independent of the social class of students.

English Language

The variables contributing to the School block in the English

---

Table 9.6: Between-school final regression analysis: English Language O-level.

Variable	Simple r	Standardized B	R^2
O/EXAMS	.87	.78	.75
SSEXM	.00	−.29	.79
EXAMS	−.52	.20	.83
SOPIN5	.14	−.15	.86
OPIN2	.80	.01	.87
WKTM	.38	−.01	.88
AGE	−.37	.03	.89
SOPIN3	.36	.04	.89
SOPIN1	.74	.09	.89
FAJOB	−.68	−.47	.89
MTEACH	−.21	.18	.90
FAEDU	−.51	.57	.90
TMSTUDY	.72	.41	.90
OTHESUB	−.39	.11	.91
FIELD	.24	.12	.91
SOPIN6	.34	.02	.91

Language analysis betray the importance of school type. In the School block the proportion that O-level examinations form of the total number of examinations offered by the school is positively and highly correlated (.87) with achievement, while there is a negative correlation (.52) for the total number of different examinations, which include CSE examinations, with achievement. The non-selective schools, necessarily catering for candidates unable to reach O-level standard, inevitably offer a larger total number of examinations than the selective schools, which concentrate on GCE. The representation of school sex, both through type of school and through proportion of male teachers, is to be expected from the sex bias of the selective schools in the sample, already reported in Chapter Three.

Even though the Parent Body block contributes a minority share to the explanation of between-school variables (52 per cent as against 92 per cent for schools), it is evident that social class, represented by levels of father's job and education, is bound up with the selective admission effect of schools. That social class is not a dominant feature is made apparent by the explanatory power, instrumental as well as statistical, of the variables in the other blocks.

The Student Body block emphasizes the positive contribution of the time spent in study and of the ability to take the examinations at an earlier age. The Teacher block indicates the benefit of teachers specializing in the teaching of English and of more time devoted to the study of the subjects. The School—Individual block offers variables which emphasize that the traditional, academic and examination oriented school, which emphasizes hard work and conformity, both in study and behaviour, is more highly achieving.

English Literature (A)

That there is something odd about the English Literature results can be seen from the very small proportion of total variance which lies between schools for this subject in contrast to all other subjects. That it is a feature of the sample rather than of the examination would appear to be supported by a comparison of the F-ratios derived by the London Board itself and for this sample. The London Board offers two syllabuses in English Literature, A and B. Of the 15 selective schools which offer candidates in either A or B, 11 chose B and one offered candidates for both syllabuses. Of the 21 non-selective schools, 12 chose A alone, five B alone and four offered candidates in both A and B. Other evidence makes it clear that English Literature A does not

Table 9.7: Between-school final regression analysis: English Literature (A) O-level.

Variable	Simple r	Standardized B	R^2
SOPIN1	.70	.41	.49
O/EXAMS	.68	.36	.60
STR2	.12	.21	.65
OPIN2	.56	.25	.69
DICTATE	−.45	−.23	.73
PT. RATIO	−.23	.27	.74
ADMISS3	−.00	−.15	.77
FAJOB	−.19	−.12	.78
PRHELP	.43	.10	.78
OTHESUB	−.50	.04	.78

behave like other subjects. It is the only subject in which the mean for non-selective schools is higher than that for selective schools. Nevertheless, the difference is small and the variance between the two sets contributes less than one per cent to the between-school variance. The variation between Maintained and non-Maintained schools contributes even less. On the whole, the regression analysis is equally uninformative. The Teacher variables surviving into the regression analysis are negatively related to the dependent variable. The teachers in higher performing schools avoided dictation and did not teach other subjects to O-level standard.

The familiar indications of academically-oriented schools being more highly achieving are present, including the number of O-level examinations offered and lower pupil—teacher ratios, but there is a contradiction of selective school effects in a positive correlation with mixed ability grouping and a dissociation from the use of parental preference in admission practice. Most exceptionally too, there is a positive correlation with parental help being given. However, the school press indicators are familiar. The schools are seen to have a reputation for academic success and to focus upon examinations.

In summary, this incoherent collection of independent variables suggests that, as a subject, English Literature differs somewhat from the remainder and that the sample is not representative. In particular, the low proportion of variance which lies between schools arises in substantial measure from the failure of English Literature A to display the same characteristics as other subjects, and, indeed, reversing the normal direction of correlation with type of school. The safest course would be to disregard this subject as contributing meaningfully to the central problems of the study.

French

It is with some surprise that one notices that despite the low proportion of between-school variance in French accounted for by the selective admission effect, the school variables surviving into the regression analyses reflect social class sources of variation and the distinction between Maintained and non-Maintained schools. It is this latter category which gives the clue to the anomaly. While the variable between selective and non-selective schools accounts for 13.95 per cent of between-school variation in achievement, the difference between the subset of selective schools that are not Maintained schools (the Independent and Direct Grant schools) and the remaining schools contributes 23.84 per cent to the between-school variance. In other words, the selective admission effect is contributed mainly by the differentiation of the subset of seven non-Maintained schools from the remainder. This division of the between-school variance must therefore be considered rather differently. The particular effect of belonging to non-Maintained schools in achieving higher performance in French may be reasonably explained by the greater opportunity that children in the

Table 9.8: Between-school final regression analysis: French O-level.

Variable	Simple r	Standardized B	R^2
FAEDU	−.70	−.58	.49
OPIN2	.59	.49	.70
SAMESUB	.57	.64	.80
RADIO	.48	.40	.85
ATTITUDE	.41	.27	.88
FRSPACE	−.48	−.29	.91
MAINTAIN	−.66	.62	.92
SES	−.67	.32	.94
QUAL	.47	.31	.94
AEXAMS	.29	−.33	.95
SOPIN7	−.32	.13	.96
FAJOB	−.68	−.08	.96
OPIN1	−.65	−.03	.96

G

higher SES groups would be expected to have to visit France and to have parents who themselves have learned French. The appearance of the number of A-level examinations taken by higher scoring schools is confirmation that these are academically oriented schools with a wide range of subjects taken in preparation for admission into higher education. It can be observed that family background achieves a high prediction value, the two Parent Body variables explaining 54 per cent of the between-school variance. Higher scoring student groups accept their peers as setting their standards and have a positive attitude towards staying on at school. Teacher variables are for the most part highly specific to the teaching of French. Candidates would appear to be better prepared by teachers who had taught the same subject to an O-level previously, who had made use of radio and who were well qualified for the teaching of French. While the presence of the School—Individual block variables must be understood as arising from the particular circumstances of the Maintained/non-Maintained dichotomy, their purport is clear; these schools are seen to emphasize a work and examination-oriented perception of school with little distraction by games or sport and with the requirement that students conform to the school rather than that the school adapt to them.

Almost all the between-school variance in French is explained by the final regression analysis and the subsequent partitioning of variance reveals that 18 per cent is uniquely contributed by the Teacher block, in contrast to the seven per cent contributed by the Parent Body block. Thus, although the effects of social class upon selective admission have been operative, they have not saturated the subsequent achievement in French. Half the explained variance is contributed by all blocks acting in concert and all but seven per cent of the other half by school-related variables.

German

We might expect exactly similar effects in German to those in French but here we must take into account the minority place of German in English secondary schools. There are fewer than 500 candidates for German but more than 1,300 candidates for French. In contrast to French, a small part, 12.56 per cent, of between-school variance in German is accounted for by the variation between non-Maintained schools and Maintained schools and the major source of variation (79 per cent) is between selective and non-selective schools in general. Thus the results in German differ from both those in English

Table 9.9: Between-school final regression analysis: German O-level.

Variable	Simple r	Standardized B	R^2
QUAL	.73	.87	.53
BTGP	.62	.24	.78
SOPIN7	−.37	−.51	.87
TSEX	.14	−.13	.92
TMSTUDY	.52	.33	.94
FAJOB	−.57	.36	.96
PUPIL16	.67	.25	.97
SOPIN1	.22	−.56	.98

Language, where the between variation for selective and non-selective schools is also high, but an even smaller proportion (1.7 per cent) of between-school variance is contributed from the non-Maintained/Maintained source, and from French which is much less influenced by the self-selective nature of the sample.

In the case of German, the variables surviving into the regression analysis do not directly identify school type. However, the selection of Admission Factor 4 as a predictor for German (Table 6.7), even though it does not appear in Table 9.9, is an indirect indication of the effect of school type. This suggests that for German, the schools whose candidates do well, provide prospectuses and have a geographically defined catchment area, admit without reference to marks and encourage parents to visit. There is a high correlation too between the number of pupils aged 16 and over and performance in German and these two school block variables taken together seem to signal Direct Grant and Grammar schools as the high performers. Certainly the School—Individual variables present such schools as traditionally academic and as requiring conformity and not emphasizing sport. The only surviving student block variable, the number of hours spent in private study, is substantially correlated with achievement. The teacher variables also confirm the traditional formality of the higher scoring schools, which have the better qualified teachers and adapt teaching to differences between groups. The low but significant contribution from teacher sex (females sex high) probably reflects the sample bias towards single sex, girls' selective schools.

The partitioning of explained between-school variance into those components attributable to blocks would seem in the case of German to identify a large contribution from the Teacher block which uniquely contributes 31 per cent. Yet, given the high selective admission component of between variance for German, it is not possible to assert a constructive collusion between teacher and other blocks. It seems more probable that the major effect arises through the selective association of teachers, school, family and individual variables at the point at which children are admitted to the schools. It is evident from the number of schools and the number of candidates contributing to the sample for German that it has a different status in the curriculum from French. The majority of Maintained schools would not include a German specialist on the staff as a matter of priority. It is more likely that a teacher whose major second language was French, but who had also included German in a first degree as a subsidiary language, would be employed. Old established schools, like Direct Grant and Independent schools, are more likely to appoint a German specialist as a matter of choice, for girls with a literary intention, for boys as a means of supporting scientific studies. It must be concluded that, while the results for German are interesting, they do not contribute much that is useful for the purposes of this study.

History (B)

Although selective admission accounts for only 18 per cent of the between-school variance in History, the small contingent of non-Maintained schools leads to 28.13 per cent of between-variance being accounted for from this source alone. Thus, we must expect social class variables to appear in the explanation of the differences between schools in History. The appearance of a negative correlation for Maintained schools as the leading surviving variable in the School block conforms with that expectation and the negative correlation with mixed ability grouping possibly arises from this source too. The positive correlation with the number of male teachers must likewise be regarded as something of an oddity of the sample rather than as a general feature of between-school variance in History. Teacher variables contributed nothing to the explanation of variance, yielding either non-significant partial correlations or leading to incompatibility with other blocks and they were therefore eliminated from the partitioning. Uncommonly, father's job does not appear among the Parent Body variables, mother's education being left to carry the implication of social status. This should not be regarded as being particularly significant for History since

Table 9.10: Between-school final regression analysis: History (B) O-level.

Variable	Simple r	Standardized B	R^2
OPIN1	−.60	−.09	.36
ATTITUDE	.49	.09	.48
STR2	−.44	−.36	.56
MAINTAIN	−.59	−.18	.63
MTEACH	.47	.43	.69
MAEDU	−.45	−.34	.72

the social class variables of father's and mother's occupation and education were constantly competing for admission in the Family block and which one survived was often a matter of accident.

The Student Body and School—Individual blocks contribute nothing extra to our knowledge of how achievement in History can be explained apart from the general features we have discussed already in relation to the other subjects. They are more a product of the school characteristics than informative in their own right. This is not at all surprising when one notices the large unique contribution of the School block and the fact that if this block were to be eliminated from the partitioning, virtually no explained variance would remain.

Geography

The non-Maintained/Maintained segment of the between-school variance is small in the case of Geography, being no more than 7.8 per cent. Thus, although we are likely to find selective admission effects corresponding with the 26 per cent of variance reported earlier, there are unlikely to be strong social class associations. The number of pupils aged 16 and over and the number of O-level examinations offered by the school are variables positively and substantially related to achievement and are confirmation of the higher performance of the selective schools. There is a small correlation with school sex being male which must be regarded as a feature of the constitution of the sample and

Table 9.11: Between-school final regression analysis: Geography O-level.

Variable	Simple r	Standardized B	R^2
O/EXAMS	.73	.47	.54
PUPIL16	.72	.38	.68
TOPIN2	.21	.37	.75
QUAL	.32	.33	.81
SSEXM	.17	−.29	.84
TMSTUDY	.58	.05	.85
FAJOB	−.57	.15	.85
SOPIN3	.44	.13	.85
OPIN3	.62	.15	.85
PROJ	−.29	−.16	.86
SOPIN6	.27	−.04	.86
SOPIN5	.37	−.05	.86

another which expresses the view of teachers in the higher scoring schools that the focus is on examinations.

Teacher variables are again specific; there is a positive correlation with level of qualification and a negative correlation with the use of project methods. The Parent Body block, as we were led to expect from the low contribution of the non-Maintained/Maintained schools division, explains a relatively small proportion of the between variance, only father's job surviving into the final analysis. The Student Body block also contains only one survivor, the time spent on private study which is positively correlated with achievement. Once again, the School—Individual block points to high achievement being associated with schools which are examination oriented and in which pupils recognize the selective character of the schools and examination success as providing enhanced chances of further study and good job prospects.

Spoken English

If the sciences are likely to lead to the detection of variables representing school-based effects upon achievement, Spoken English would be expected to represent much more of social background. It has already been shown that 31.67 per cent of between variance can be accounted for by the selective/non-selective division between schools and it would be conceivable that the difference between Maintained and non-Maintained schools could be even greater. The sample is such,

Table 9.12: Between-school final regression analysis: Spoken English O-level.

Variable	Simple r	Standardized B	R^2
PUPIL16	.77	.30	.59
OPIN1	−.72	−.40	.75
TAPE	.30	.60	.85
SOPIN5	.27	.34	.88
OPIN3	.31	.26	.92
AGE	−.15	−.03	.93
PROJ	.26	−.24	.94
SOPIN3	.31	−.18	.94
BTIND	.51	−.19	.95
DICTATE	−.63	−.31	.96
STRIP	.07	.05	.96
FAEDU	−.52	−.43	.96
TMSTUDY	.72	−.60	.97
PT.RATIO	−.18	.17	.97
MAINTAIN	−.52	−.08	.97

however, that only 6.36 per cent of the variance is attributable to this component. Thus, while association with selective admission effects can be expected, social class ought to be less in evidence in the regression analyses than in the case of the sciences. It would be noted that only 181 of the 1,165 children who took Spoken English came from non-Maintained schools. In Chemistry, there were 94 out of 461 and in Physics 123 out of 550. It seems possible, therefore, that the absence of a social class bias may be a function of the constitution of the sample rather than of the non-intervention of the social class function in the successful completion of the curriculum.

The partitioning of explained variance between blocks only partly supports this viewpoint. The greater part of the common between-variance is attributable to Teacher, School and School—Individual blocks, while the Parent Body block has the lowest contribution of any. The variables surviving from the School block into the regression analysis are indicative of the features one might expect. There is a high correlation of achievement with the number of pupils of age 16 and over and a low but negative correlation with pupil—teacher ratio, features which mark out the selective schools. However, despite the constitution of the sample there is a substantial negative correlation with being in a Maintained school, implying that social class does have an effect. We have already noted that 84 per cent of the candidates are girls and that 63 per cent of them come from selective schools. The fact that 539 of tthe 1,165 candidates came from single sex selective girls' schools reinforces the view that it is mainly selective girls' schools that are making the difference.

The Teacher block makes the largest contribution and it is apparent from the nature of the variables that it is the operations of teaching that are discriminating. There are positive correlations with audio-visual aid usage, including film strip and tape and with project methods and adaptation to individual differences. There is a strong negative correlation with dictation as a technique of student preparation. From the Family block, only father's education survives into the regression analysis and it accounts for only 27 per cent of the between-school variance. From the Student Body block comes direct evidence of the result of work input. The correlation between the amount of time spent in personal study and success in the examination is 0.72 for Spoken English. There is a small negative correlation with age which marks out the more academic schools which enter younger candidates. The variables in the School—Individual block portray the higher scoring schools as being examination-oriented and as making study important for all pupils, but as intolerant of less academic pupils and not encouraging self-expression.

B. Advanced level examinations

In only four of the examination subjects that might have been taken at A-level were the numbers of candidates sufficient to justify application of the regression analyses. Even then, in the case of Mathematics, the number of students did not reach 200. Candidates were drawn from between 20 and 22 schools, but at this stage there were no Modern schools left in the sample. Once again, the greater part of the variance lay within schools, the proportion between schools ranging between 12 and 32 per cent. Each examination subject will be interpreted separately in the same manner as for the O-level subjects.

Pure Mathematics

Pidgeon (1967) reports that the largest source of variation in the A-level students' Mathematics scores was type of school, so it would be reasonable to expect that, when positively selective schools are compared with the remainder, a high proportion of variance would be

Table 9.13: Between-school final regression analysis: Pure Mathematics A-level.

Variable	Simple r	Standardized B	R^2
SAPASS	.90	.59	.81
SOPIN2	−.63	−.12	.87
IPACE	.00	.17	.91
FAJOB	−.41	−.30	.93
DIRGRANT	.48	.10	.94
JOBCMP	.10	.36	.94
WKTM	.45	.12	.95
PUPIL16	.53	−.23	.95
BTGP	−.20	.30	.96
TCHEXP2	−.68	−.24	.96
SOPIN4	−.29	.13	.96
MAEDU	−.18	−.13	.96
ALVLTOT	.21	.02	.97
SOPIN3	.28	.16	.97
PROJ	.41	.11	.97
COMPREHEN	−.49	−.05	.97

accounted for. Eighteen per cent of total variance is reported by Pidgeon to be attributable to type of school. In the present study, however, between-school variance, which itself is just over 12 per cent of total variance, does not appear to be explained by selective intake factors. The proportion of between-school variance which is ascribable to the difference between positively and negatively selective schools is only 2.6 per cent, while that ascribable to the difference between Maintained and non-Maintained schools is less than one per cent.

It appears that we should look to other factors in order to account for the between-school variance, 97 per cent of which was explained by the regression analyses. Just as the within-variance contribution is entirely from the Individual block, so the explanation of between-variance is dominated by the Student Body block, 17.4 per cent uniquely and 74.6 per cent shared with other blocks. Schools emerge as sharing 5.9 per cent and the School—Individual block 48.4 per cent.

Only three variables survive from the Teacher block and the positive contributions are from 'number of terms spent on the course' and 'teaching through projects'. Despite the negative sign, there is also a positive contribution from 'teaching to meet between-group differences'. These are meaningful teaching variables and suggest that specialized teachers are at work. The failure of selective and Maintained/non-Maintained factors to account for between-school variance should not mislead us into supposing that type of school has no effect; the variables surviving into the School block indicate otherwise. Being a Direct Grant school carried a positive correlation, and being a Comprehensive school carried a negative correlation. Both are of sufficient size to indicate their importance. An even higher simple correlation is achieved by the variable, 'number of pupils aged 16 and over'. This suggests that the schools which retain pupils beyond school-leaving age in greater numbers are likely to achieve higher results.

The contribution of the Parent Body block (42.6 per cent) looks small against that of the Student Body block considered alone, to which 89 per cent of the variance would have been assigned if partitioning had not been adopted. One variable contributes the greatest proportion to this variance — the students' own estimate of the level of success they will achieve. There is a positive contribution too from the total number of A-levels taken, which suggests that these high achievers are not specializing in only one subject. The substantial correlation, negative in direction, between achievement and teacher expectation in the worst subject suggests that the standards which students adopt are related to the standards operative in their school. The two remaining variables make a small contribution and can be virtually neglected. The three variables in the School—Individual block imply that higher scoring pupils reject the idea that the school is not selective and that discipline is not strict; the pupils also assert that behaviour is of more importance to the school than achievement, although petty rules are not imposed.

The overall picture is much the same as we have observed in the O-level analyses, in which the higher scores are achieved by the more selective schools, which draw pupils of higher socioeconomic status, who have a realistic confidence in their likelihood of being successful in their examinations, and regard their schools as being mainly concerned with making this possible.

English Literature
The mean of the scores in English Literature of the positively selective schools is 50.2 as against 47.8 for the negatively selective

Table 9.14: Between-school final regression analysis: English Literature A-level.

Variable	Simple r	Standardized B	R^2
FRSPACE	−.62	−.20	.38
TOPIN2	−.49	−.16	.68
YEARS	−.23	−.32	.81
SOPIN6	.32	−.14	.85
HMHELP	−.44	−.48	.89
FAJOB	−.12	−.29	.92
ATTITUDE	.21	.24	.93
TV	−.50	−.73	.95
TRAIN	−.25	−.35	.96
FAMPACE	.50	−.15	.97
TOPIN1	−.24	−.38	.97
YREXP	.05	.24	.98
IPACE	.37	−.17	.99
OPIN2	.19	.15	.99
SAPASS	.45	.08	.99
SOPIN4	−.25	.07	.99

schools. Nevertheless, the difference contributes only six per cent to the between-school variance and the difference between the non-Maintained schools and Maintained schools, while in the accustomed direction contributes only 9.7 per cent. The teachers in the higher scoring schools perceive their schools as having ideal characteristics. They see their schools as preparing students for later study more than for examinations, regard pupils as important even if they do not achieve good examination results, and believe that candidates do not feel under pressure from the school to do well in examinations. Likewise they do not think that examinations limit what is taught and regard teaching as not being mainly concerned with getting children through examinations. The higher scoring schools are also less likely to have organized children into lower, middle and upper schools.

The teachers of English Literature in the higher scoring schools are distinguished in their block as rarely using television transmissions and as not having received training in the subject they are teaching. There is also a small positive correlation with number of years of experience. Two of the three variables in the Parent Body block indicate that the candidates in the higher scoring schools do not perceive the family as setting the standards for their work or as giving direct help. These two together may be indicative of a middle-class family background, where motivation comes from the parents' interest but where parental help is either not needed or not available. The positive relationship with the status of the father's job contributes to this interpretation. It is further reinforced when we consider the Student Body block where the highest single correlation, which is positive in sense, relates to 'friends setting the standard for one's work' while 'setting one's own standards' is negatively correlated. Apart from these, there are positive correlations with expected level of success and with attitude towards school. The School–Individual block paints much the same picture as we have had so far, with the higher scoring candidates perceiving the school as being free from the application of petty rules; hard work is not seen as being necessary for success, although students do recognize that teacher opinion is authoritative.

There is rather more between-school variance in English Literature than in Mathematics, 22 per cent of total variance, and almost all of this is accounted for by the regression analyses. Little is contributed uniquely by any block and, in keeping with the interpretation given above, the School block shares with others the highest proportion, 56 per cent. Student Body and Teacher blocks come next and are followed by Parent Body and School–Individual blocks. It would seem that by this stage in the study of English Literature, a liberal sentiment is conducive to achievement and finds its most appropriate context in school communities which are less restrictive in their ethos. It is worth noting in the partitioning of variance that the composite of School and Teacher blocks uniquely explains all the between-school variance.

French

Twenty per cent of total variance in French lies between schools and 94 per cent of between variance is explained by the blocks in concert. However, the contribution of the Parent Body block is extremely small, 8.4 per cent, and, as in the case of English Literature, the largest contribution comes from the School block closely followed by the Teacher block. The Parent Body block is not far behind and even the School–Individual block contributes, in common with others, 31.4 per cent. There is, furthermore, a unique contribution of 13.6 per cent from the Teacher block. Teacher and School blocks uniquely share 22.4 per cent, which is only surpassed when blocks of Student Body and

School—Individual variables are combined with them and achieve 30.7 per cent.

Little of this contribution from schools is attributable to selective features. The mean of the positively selective schools is 52.23 and of the non-selective schools, 52.19. The variance contributed by this difference is less than one per cent of between-school variance. Likewise the difference between Maintained and non-Maintained schools accounts for only 4.5 per cent. We would, therefore, expect some direct indication from Teacher and School blocks as to the nature of the difference. One teacher variable, which has a substantial simple correlation with achievement, suggests that the school operates through differentiating between groups in terms of ability. Teaching is said to be directed at differences between groups. There is also a positive correlation with the use of a project approach to the teaching of French.

Table 9.15: Between-school final regression analysis: French A-level.

Variable	Simple r	Standardized B	R^2
BTGP	.65	1.76	.43
PROJ	.32	−1.15	.78
TCHEXP 2	−.30	−.34	.87
SOPIN 2	.21	.29	.94

Among the School—Individual variables, there is a positive correlation between achievement and the school being regarded as having a reputation for academic success. At the Student Body level, students' perceptions of teachers as having a high opinion of them in their worst subject correlate positively with achievement.

Geography

More than 32 per cent of total variance in Geography achievement lies between schools. Of this between-variance, 26.8 per cent can be explained by the variation between Maintained and non-Maintained schools. The mean score for non-Maintained schools was 52.75, while that for Maintained schools was 45.02. Similarly 91.8 per cent of variance lay between positively selective and negatively selective schools

Table 9.16: Between-school final regression analysis: Geography A-level.

Variable	Simple r	Standardized B	R^2
SOPIN5	.71	.24	.51
FRSPACE	−.57	−.15	.79
FAEDU	−.58	−.04	.86
SAPASS	.26	.12	.90
O/EXAMS	.71	.30	.93
GRAMMAR	−.28	−.25	.94
COMPREHEN	−.54	.05	.94
OPIN1	−.65	−.11	.96
PROJ	−.20	−.49	.97
AEXAMS	.34	.26	.98
SOPIN4	−.24	−.32	.99
OPIN2	.14	.22	1.00
FAMPACE	.44	.15	1.00

with differences in the expected direction.

Once again, almost all this variance was explained by the regression analyses, by far the greater part of it being shared by the School with other blocks. The School—Individual block shared almost as much, followed by the Teacher block, then the Parent Body and Student Body blocks. The most informative of the partitioning analyses relates to the combination of the School, Student Body and School—Individual blocks, yielding uniquely 23.8 per cent of variance, and the combination of the Teacher, School and School—Individual blocks yielding 20.5 per cent uniquely. The first variable entered in the final regression analysis represents an opinion of the school held by the students and in itself accounts for over 50 per cent of variance. It confirms the impression gained of the effects of selective and non-Maintained schools, in that students in the higher scoring schools recognize that the schools discriminate in favour of bright pupils and are not enjoyable (they impose the wearing of uniform!). The second variable represents a strong acknowledgement of friends setting the standard for one's work. The first two variables alone account for 79 per cent of the between-school variance. That it is the Direct Grant and Independent schools that are being identified is shown by the positive correlation with the number of O- and A-level examinations taken by candidates from the school and by the negative correlation with Grammar and Comprehensive types of school. The Parent Body block shares a substantial proportion of between variance, 47.8 per cent, with only two variables, the first being the level of father's education and the second a denial that the family sets the standard for work.

Conclusion

In reviewing the analyses of the 11 O-level and four A-level subjects one must confess to some disappointment that, even at this level of pre-selection in which we are dealing with students in the top 50 per cent of the ability range, after at least 11 years in school, much of the differences in achievement between schools are to be explained by the level of selection for admission to secondary schools. On the whole, there is sufficient evidence that family background is less important than the individual ability of the student. Even where family social class has been instrumental in determining the schools to which children go and this has resulted in higher achievement, student ability at the point of admission would appear to be concomitant. Thus, in the main, schools make the difference by responding to the abilities of the students and there is a tendency amongst this set of English schools for the better qualities of teaching and school facilities to find their way to the schools with the children of higher ability. The process is collusive, but positively so. There is evidence in some subjects that the qualities of teaching, in particular, make a difference to achievement, even beyond what would be expected from the abilities of the students.

In general, the characteristics of schools which are emphasized by the analyses as contributing to achievement are representative of a more conservative and, some would believe, reactionary view of education. Time and again we find that the schools which are associated with superior achievement are those which are work and examination oriented, in which students work hard spending considerable time in study and which are successful in retaining students at the higher levels of the school. It would be a grave mistake, however, to regard such conclusions as supportive of a return to a more repressive education. Rather, perhaps, one should take seriously the view that schools are in a special position in relation to society; that they are not mirrors of the changing liberality of society but perform best the function that society wishes when they remain at some distance from the looser control which now characterizes parental child-rearing practices and impose a formality against which students find themselves partly in conflict but which serves to set the standards to which they aspire.

Chapter Ten

Conclusions

Despite the deceptive eclecticism of the analytic model and the contrived homogeneity of the sample used in the present study, the investigation is neither atheoretical nor tendentious. It incorporates the proposition that variance in the achievements of pupils can be explained by four main blocks of variables and a fifth which is distinguished because it is jointly assignable to two of the other blocks. The design of the analysis avoids the imposition of structure upon the relationship between the blocks, not because the study is atheoretical, but explicitly to enable competing hypotheses to be tested.

Without wishing to labour the theoretical framework of the study, its principal features are as follows. Firstly, home background influences (heritable factors and the formative influences of early rearing) exercise their main effects before a child enters formal school and largely determine readiness for learning. Secondly, schools accept a principle of equality of concern for all pupils in which equal values, but not identical components, of school-based resources are available to each child. Thirdly, educational policies are concerned with ways of assigning resources to schools which will maximize desirable outcomes for students. Amongst the desirable outcomes is positive, academic achievement. In general, the ability of a school to change its resources is limited. Some resources are more malleable than others; for example, teacher qualification and school curricula are easier to change than school buildings or the social class composition of schools. Fourthly, differences amongst the achievements of children at any level of education will be associated with differences in learning readiness, which will have been substantially determined by the learner's history. Schools do relatively little to change the correlation between readiness and achievement. Finally, when the *level* of education offered is such that the learner's prior history (familial and school) determines those who will be admitted to it, then social class of family will cease to exert an important influence amongst the survivors. Differences in achievement at this stage will be largely attributable to differences amongst students in their academic inclination and their personality and character and to differences between schools in their quality of instruction and/or possession and disposition of resources. Since quality of instruction and school resources are interdependent in disposition, they will account for achievement in concert rather than individually.

The design of this study depended upon choosing a level of education in England at which survival would have eliminated the differentiating effects of familial factors. The study would then be mainly concerned with the question of what differences between schools in achievement were explicable by differences in their quality and/or resources. It is important to an understanding of the study to recognize that in choosing Ordinary level of the General Certificate of Education as the minimal level of achievement necessary for inclusion in the study, selective effects were deliberately accepted. Our sample is inevitably one of children who are likely to be in the top 50 per cent of achievers in their cohort. In 1972–73, 128,330 of the 416,360 of school leavers had taken no O-levels (308 per thousand). Three hundred and seventy per thousand took no more than one subject, 416 per thousand took no more than two subjects. Of the 288,030 students who took at least one O-level subject, 201,910 or 701 per thousand, took five or more O-levels, which is 484 per thousand of school leavers. Thus at the age of about 16 years, when O-levels are taken, most of the selective variables arising from family background and prior educational background will already have taken effect. It follows that within our sample, family background will only exercise such degree of support for commitment to O-levels as the nature of the interaction between home and school permits. We should not, therefore, expect a strong unique effect of family background factors. This applies to between-school differences as well as to within-school differences.

Given the large between-school differences in social class reported in the chapter on sampling, it is clear that social class is likely to be confounded with other variables. If higher social class increases the likelihood of a student going to a selective or Independent school and survival into O-level increases that selectivity, then social class will be commensurate with teacher and school provision and with academic ability. One might say that between-school differences are largely pre-determined by the earlier selective effects, so that we should not be surprised to find a large proportion of between-school achievement variance explained, and that, by the collusive effect of all blocks of variables.

One is forced to question whether it could be otherwise. It would be possible if one can imagine a total failure of the schools and teachers to adapt to the nature of individual and social differences amongst their students. In such circumstances, only the Parent Body and Student Body blocks would contribute, and nothing would be shared with the School Block. We might also envisage an ordered variation in school and teacher facilities correlated with the ordered variation of social class and individual blocks, but irrelevant to variation in achievement.* In that case, the explained variance would be largely shared, but the Parent Body and Student Body blocks would contribute a somewhat larger share of explained variation. Likewise, the School—Individual block, reflecting as it does, the prevailing ethos of the school as an academic community and expressing the adaptive properties of the school, would be expected to make a large shared contribution to achievement variance, since ordered, although irrelevant, school and teacher provision would permit systematic variation with achievement. Thus alternative hypotheses could be entertained. The results are not predetermined by the structure of the sample.

We now may return to the questions with which the study began. We shall consider each question in turn and attempt to summarize our findings.

Question 1. Are the contributions of schools — their curricula, their resources, their organization, their teaching — to differences in achievement, greater than those suggested by the Equality of Educational Opportunity Study (EEOS), when examinations, focussed on prescribed curricula, replace objective tests of academic aptitude as the criterion measures?

Objective, structural questions, short answer and essay type exam-

---

* For example, differences between schools might be a function only of attitude towards games, social manners or religious practices.

inations were all embodied in the set of O and A level examinations studied. It is apparent from the discussion of them that the form of examination paper was adapted to the characteristics of the curriculum, no attempt being made to impose multiple-choice questions for the whole of an examination subject nor to adopt them because of administrative convenience. The main benefit of this approach, as compared with that of the EEOS, has been that we are dealing with measures as criteria which the schools accept as the targets for their curricula and which the students recognize as coincident with the objectives of academic motivation. It should be emphasized that the study is not seeking to weigh the constraints implied by the psychometric formulations of objective tests against the proneness to error of the more liberal, long-essay type of examination. Indeed, evidence is presented supporting the reliability of the more conventional (*i.e.*, essay) examinations.

Statistical analyses demonstrate that under these examination conditions, between-school variance is a larger proportion of total variance than the findings of the EEOS would have led us to expect. Certainly, so far as the central point of this question is concerned, almost all between-school variance is explained and schools do indeed share a much larger contribution to the explanation of variance than in the EEOS. The nature of these effects will be discussed in answer to question three.

Question 2. When the sample of students studied is more homogeneous in level of educational survival than that for the Equality of Educational Opportunity Survey (EEOS), are the school and teacher effects more in evidence?

Evidence has been presented that, at least in terms of survival into a deliberately academic curriculum, the students under study are indeed more homogeneous than those of the EEOS who at the secondary level ran the full spectrum of curricular tracks. It is to the partitioning of between-school explained variance that we should turn for an answer to the question. School effects are particularly obtrusive in the type of selectivity exercised by schools at the point of admission. Thus, in terms of a maintained/non-maintained and academically selective/non-selective source of variation in admission, the effect upon achievement is substantial. Because of this it has not been possible to distinguish the effects of level of ability at the point of admission and level of SES from the effects of school type alone. So far as social class is concerned, it would seem that the comparatively subordinate contribution made by the Parent Body block is only partly attributable to the confounding with type of school, since such contribution as it makes is shared with all other blocks.

In only one Ordinary level subject (Chemistry) is the total contribution (unique and common) of the Parent Body block higher than that of the School or the Teacher block. In eight of the 11 subjects, 80 per cent of the explained variance is ascribable in the form of unique plus common components to the School or the Teacher block, while for no subject is this true in the case of the Parent Body block. For no subject does the unique contribution of the Parent Body block exceed seven per cent, whereas in the case of the Teacher block, its unique contribution does so for four subjects and in the case of the School block for seven subjects. The size of the unique contributions of the Teacher and School blocks is often substantial, but in only one instance is it higher than the shared contribution.

The variables which survive to represent schools and teachers point clearly to the way in which these schools and teachers make their greater contribution. They do so in association with the other blocks but nevertheless have their individual character particularly in terms of type of school. While the teacher variables include reference to supposed virtues amongst teachers such as qualifications and length of experience, it is the operative teaching variables which are usually to the fore. The amount of time spent on the course, the adjustment of teaching to the specific characteristics of the subjects and the belief of teachers in the worthwhileness of an examination-goal-oriented approach, which does not seriously limit the curricular choice, are perhaps amongst the most specific indications of the ways in which teachers' influences are operative.

Question 3. When the unique contributions to achievement variance of families, individuals, schools and teachers are separated from the contributions they make in common, does the family influence loom so large as would be expected from the Equality of Educational Opportunity Survey (EEOS)?

This is one question to which the study can give a definite answer. The unique contributions of all but the Teacher and School blocks in the between-schools analyses were found to be negligible. In the within-school analyses, the Individual block alone completely dwarfed any contribution that might have been made by the family. However, even the Teacher and School blocks contributed more to the explanation of variance in concert with other blocks than they did uniquely. This apparent lack of clarity must be held to be less a disadvantage of the strategy of decomposition of variance than of the conceptual limitations underlying the assignment of variables to blocks. It would seem that when we wish to explain the differences between schools in achievement, we cannot expect a neat division of effects into the relatively simple or formal entities which are conventionally seen as agents in the achievement production process.

Question 4. If indicators of school, individual and teacher attributes are replaced by measures of the processes, attitudes and values of the agents, do such measures increase the predictive power of the independent variables?

Once again this can be answered without qualification. The presence of these measures does increase the amount of achievement variance which can be explained; moreover, they achieve considerable importance. Such variables occur principally in the Teacher block, the Student Body block and the School—Individual block. The teachers' and the pupils' views of the selective admission character of the school, of its examination orientation and of the importance of work coincide. Additionally, the high predictive value of some of the variables in the Student Body block demonstrate that the students' expectations of success in the examinations were realistic. The fact that they had such a clear idea of their likelihood of success, while not itself a subject of enquiry, must indicate that there was sufficient feedback from the teachers to enable them to make that estimation. The power of these variables was such that in the first partitioning analyses they obscured the contribution of other blocks, since they were virtually surrogates for the dependent variables. In the final Ordinary-level analyses they were removed.

Likewise, the inclusion of such variables permitted us to recognize that students are more likely to achieve high scores when they are enrolled in schools which they regard as examination-oriented, and that in these same schools, students claim it is their friends rather than their parents or teachers who set the standards for their work. In general the School—Individual block, which contains measures of attitudes, values and perceptions, extends the explanatory power of the study and leads to information concerning the working of schools that would have been inaccessible if only static indicators had been used.

Conclusions   199

All four of the questions posed in the introduction can be answered affirmatively and none of the outcomes of the study contradicts the theoretical framework we adopted. However, in looking back over what we have done we are led to wonder whether survey research of this kind has not reached the limits of its explanatory capability. So far as policy issues are concerned we have not been able to point to a single variable which is easily, no matter how expensively, capable of being altered by an administrative act or by the supply of increased funds which will unequivocally raise school achievement. What we have done is to show that schools do make a difference, even if we have not demonstrated that this is in the direction of reducing social inequality, and that they accomplish this within a socioeconomic process to which they are also subject.

Here we may consider briefly problems which arise if the concept of equality of educational opportunity as a goal for schools is taken to mean that schools should accept as a cardinal principle of their operation the reduction of differences in educational achievements between socioeconomic groups (Coleman, 1968). The concept of socioeconomic class in itself creates problems. Socioeconomic status is a construct and indices of status serve to represent that construct insofar as they measure the quality of the home as a large part of the environment in which a child is reared, but they are only descriptive indices which aggregate together such diverse features as the esteem in which the father's occupation is held, the level of family income, the intellectual competence of the parent, the expectations and aspirations of the family for the child, the attitudes of the parents towards school and to work and leisure, as well as the material and cultural facilities which the home offers. Thus an index of socioeconomic status may be a relatively simple and effective summary of many factors related to the education, both formal and non-formal, of a child, but in itself it offers little guidance for social or educational policy.

It seems clear that pre-school factors (heritable factors together with formative influences of early rearing) exercise substantial effects upon learning readiness before the child ever enters school. Such effects pre-dispose the interaction of the child with schools to a degree which the school, under present conditions, seems to have only limited powers to modify. To accept as paramount the task of adjusting differences between socioeconomic groups, schools would have to substitute the treatment of children by reference to their socioeconomic status for treatment according to learning and achievement characteristics, in which equal concern is given to all children, irrespective of socio-economic conditions. It is probably true to say that, at present, most teachers and schools accept a principle of equality of concern for all pupils. This does not mean, however, that identical components of school-based resources are available to each child. Each school will provide different treatments for children who appear different in their readiness for learning, and such differences in treatment as are continued to be judged necessary at successive decision points in the school system.

Even if schools were to accept a principle of treatment according to socioeconomic status, it is unlikely that, in practice, they would be able to operate it. A school has a fixed and interdependent set of resources to manage and dispose among pupils. These resources include its teachers, its space, its curricula, its time, its media and its corporate body of teachers, students and parents, all in interaction. Only certain of these resources are directly manipulable. A particular school is normally confined in terms of the number and quality of teachers it has to manage, the space and total facilities available for teaching and the total time available for learning. It must usually accept the corporate body of students and the entailed parental body as being largely beyond its own control. Even the curriculum it offers may be fixed by outside groups, such as examination boards. It is in the management of these relatively fixed resources that schools have the possibility of differing from one another in the reduction of differences in achieve-ment between socioeconomic groups. It is much more likely, however, that the differences between schools will arise from the allocation of resources which are least easily manipulable by educational policies. Insofar as schools are embedded in the communities they serve, one of their most important resources — the student and parental body — will be beyond their powers to control. Attempts to control the con-stitution of the student body in the school according to some principle of mixing have notoriously met with opposition from the community. It seems that the extent to which such mixing is tolerable may depend, in the end, less upon the resolution of cultural conflicts than upon the extent to which they permit schools to attend appropriately to the learning needs of every child.

As our system of education operates at present, once schooling has begun for a child, the interaction between his readiness to learn and the school's capability for assisting that learning substantially sets the pattern of achievement for the future. For the most part, achievement is positively correlated with readiness for learning at the point of beginning school, even though that achievement is measured some 12 years later (*cf.* Bloom, 1964).

When systems of education are such that transfer of children from one level of education to another is made without reference to their achievement we would expect subsequent differences in achievement to occur largely as a within-school phenomenon. This is not to say that in a non-selective system, differences between schools in intake do not occur. In the comprehensive American school system, for example, the social composition of high schools markedly reflects the occupational structure of the community they serve (Ramsøy, 1967); since communities differ in occupational structure, so too will the characteristics of students entering school. In this situation, we would expect that differences between schools would, to a large extent, be a function of the geographic distribution of the population and of educational policies regarding catchment areas.

This is not to say that other forms of selection do not take place in comprehensive systems. At the high school level, in particular, selection to classes and tracks occurs and groups of students within the school are treated differentially. Had Coleman *et al.* (1966) used the class rather than the school as their unit of analysis, we feel they would have found evidence for such selection and differential treatment in the form of greater variance in achievement between classes than between schools (*cf.* Kellaghan, Madaus and Rakow, 1976; Rakow, Airasian and Madaus, 1978).

When a system of education permits achievement at one level to determine the school to which a child goes at the next level, as happens in more overtly selective systems, then we would expect even greater difference in subsequent achievement between schools to arise. Furthermore, to the extent that children with different initial achievement are allocated to schools which are differentially equipped to meet their needs, greater between-school variance in achievement might be expected to arise in later than in earlier assessments. Human nature being as it is, the higher level of initial achievement is likely in these conditions to attract better resources and to be more sharply focussed on subsequent achievement. Thus, an analysis which attempted to distinguish those features of schools which contribute to their differences in achievement would be bound to reflect interaction between students' characteristics and school resources. It would be unlikely that any single feature (*e.g.*, family background or school facility) would be found to be uniquely responsible for any large part of between-school variance, since all the factors would be collusive and would share their contribution to variance.

In conclusion, we may note that schools would appear to function best in terms of academic achievement when they can select a goal external to themselves, examinations, with which they can identify their internal processes and towards which end they selectively admit. That society rewards the achievement of these goals reinforces their status and confirms them in the belief of their practices. It is not necessary for the student body to be in direct sympathy with the practices of a school for the school to achieve its goals. Inevitably, there is competitive benefit and for every student who passes his examination and succeeds there are others who do not enjoy the privilege of being in the same kind of school, but it cannot be taken as self-evident that the appropriate attitudes of lower achieving schools should be to reject examination goals and to substitute others.

To the extent that a desire to continue in school implies a positive attitude towards school, our study shows that differences between schools in such attitudes of students are explained by the regression equations in much the same way that achievement is explained. The fostering of positive attitudes does not appear to be an alternative policy to that of encouraging academic success, in that their occurrence is coincident and in that they depend on similar parameters for their explanation.

Finally, our findings suggest that insofar as schools are led by the existence of examinations, which make a difference to a student's future, to mobilize the best of their resources to maximize the best that each student has to offer and to be adaptive in doing so, then examinations may turn out not to be irrelevant to personal and social adjustment and the collusion between all the factors leading to individual differences may be socially realistic.

References

AVERCH, H.A., CARROLL, S.J., DONALDSON, T.S., KIESLING, H.J., and PINCUS, J. (1972) *How Effective is Schooling? A critical review and synthesis of research findings.* Santa Monica, California: Rand Corporation.

BARKER LUNN, J.C. (1970). *Streaming in the Primary School.* Slough: National Foundation for Educational Research.

BEATON, A.E. (1973). Commonality. Unpublished manuscript.

BEATON, A.E. (1974). Multivariate commonality analysis. In: MAYESKE, G.W., BEATON, A.E., WISLER, C.E., OKADA, T. and COHEN, W.M. *Technical Supplement to 'A Study of the Achievement of our Nation's Students.'* Washington, D.C.: U.S. Department of Health, Education and Welfare.

BENSON, C. *et al.*, (1965). *State and Local Fiscal Relationships in Public Education in California.* Report on the Senate Fact Finding Committee on Revenue and Taxation, Senate of the State of California, Sacramento.

BIDWELL, C.E. (1973). 'The social psychology of teaching.' In: TRAVERS, R.M.W. (Ed) *Second Handbook of Research on Teaching.* Chicago: Rand McNally.

BLOOM, B.S. (1956). *Taxonomy of Educational Objectives: The classification of educational goals. Handbook 1. Cognitive domain.* New York: McKay.

BLOOM, B.S. (1964). *Stability and Change in Human Characteristics.* New York: Wiley.

BLOOM, B.S. (1966). 'Twenty-five years of educational research.' *American Educational Research Journal*, 3, 211–221.

BURKHEAD, J., FOX, T.G., and HOLLAND, J.W. (1967). *Input and Output in Large City High Schools.* Syracuse, N.Y.: Syracuse University Press.

CARVER, R.P. (1974). 'Two dimensions of tests: psychometric and edumetric.' *American Psychologist*, 29, 512–518.

COHEN, D.K. (1970). 'Politics and research: Evaluation of social action programs in education.' *Review of Educational Research*, 40, 213–238.

COHEN, D.K. (1972). 'Compensatory education.' In: WALBERG, H.J. and KOPAN, A.T. (Eds) *Rethinking Urban Education* San Francisco: Jossey-Bass.

COHEN, D.K. and GARET, M.S. (1975). 'Reforming educational policy with applied social research.' *Harvard Educational Review*, 45, 17—43.

COLEMAN, J.S. (1968). 'The concept of equality of educational opportunity.' *Harvard Educational Review*, 38, 7—22.

COLEMAN, J.S. (1972). 'The evaluation of Equality of Educational Opportunity'. In: MOSTELLER, F. and MOYNIHAN, D.P. (Eds) *On Equality of Educational Opportunity*. Papers deriving from the Harvard University faculty seminar on the Coleman report. New York: Vintage Books.

COLEMAN, J.S. (1975a). 'Methods and results in the IEA studies of effects of school on learning.' *Review of Educational Research*, 45, 335—386.

COLEMAN, J.S. (1975b). 'What is meant by "an equal educational opportunity"?' *Oxford Review of Education*, 1, 27—29.

COLEMAN, J.S., CAMPBELL, E.Q., HOBSON, C.J., McPARTLAND, J., MOOD, A.M., WEINFELD, F.D., and YORK, R.L. (1966). *Equality of Educational Opportunity*. Washington D.C.: Office of Education, U.S. Department of Health, Education and Welfare.

COMBER, L.C. and KEEVES, J.P. (1973). *Science Education in Nineteen Countries. An empirical study.* New York: Wiley.

COOK, D.L. and LANGE, R. (1975). 'Limitations of educational and social policy evaluation.' *Journal of Research and Development in Education*, 8, 92—100.

CREAGER, J.A. (1971). 'Orthogonal and nonorthogonal methods for partitioning regression variance.' *American Educational Research Journal*, 8, 671—676.

CRONBACH, L.J. (1975). 'Five decades of public controversy over mental testing.' *American Psychologist*, 30, 1—14.

DYER, H.S. (1968). 'School factors and equal educational opportunity.' *Harvard Educational Review*, 38, 38—56.

FINN, J.D. (1972). Multivariance: Univariate and multivariate analysis of variance, covariance and regression. Ann Arbor, Michigan: National Educational Resources.

FOSHAY, A.W. (Ed) (1962). *Educational Achievement of Thirteen-year Olds in Twelve Countries.* Hamburg: UNESCO Institute for Education.

GETZELS, J.W. (1969). Paradigms and practices: On the contribution of research to education. Address to American Educational Research Association Annual Meeting, Los Angeles.

GOODMAN, S.M. (1959). The assessment of school quality. Albany, N.Y.: New York State Education Department.

GREAT BRITAIN: DEPARTMENT OF EDUCATION AND SCIENCE (1967). *Children and their Primary Schools.* A report of the Central Advisory Council for Education (England). London: Her Majesty's Stationery Office.

HANUSHEK, E.A. and KAIN, J.F. (1972). 'On the value of Equality of Educational Opportunity as a guide to public policy.' In: MOSTELLER, F. and MOYNIHAN, D.P. (eds) *On Equality of Educational Opportunity*. Papers deriving from the Harvard University faculty seminar on the Coleman report. New York: Vintage Books.

HUSEN, T. (1967). *International Study of Achievement in Mathematics: A comparison of twelve countries*. Volume II. Stockholm: Almqvist and Wiksell.

JENCKS, C.S. (1972a). 'The Coleman report and the conventional wisdom.' In: MOSTELLER, F. and MOYNIHAN, D.P. (Eds) *On Equality of Educational Opportunity*. Papers deriving from the Harvard University faculty seminar on the Coleman report. New York: Vintage Books.

JENCKS, C.S. (1972b). 'The quality of the data collected by *The Equality of Educational Opportunity* survey.' In: MOSTELLER, F. and MOYNIHAN, D.P. (Eds) *On Equality of Educational Opportunity*. Papers deriving from the Harvard University faculty seminar on the Coleman report. New York: Vintage Books.

JENCKS, C.S. SMITH, M., ACLAND, H., BANE, M.J., COHEN, D., GINTIS, H., HEYNS, B., and MICHELSON, S. (1972). *Inequality: A reassessment of the effect of family and schooling in America*. New York: Basic Books.

JOE, G.W. and ANDERSON, H.E. (1969). 'Mean differences and association.' *Multivariate Behavioural Research*, 4, 379–388.

KELLAGHAN, T. (1977). 'Measuring school effectiveness.' In: SUMNER, R. (Ed) *Monitoring National Standards of Attainment in Schools*. Slough: National Foundation for Educational Research.

KELLAGHAN, T., MADAUS, G.F., and RAKOW, E.A. (1976). The effects of using different units of analysis in estimating school effectiveness. Unpublished manuscript. Educational Research Centre, St. Patrick's College, Dublin.

KERLINGER, F.N. and PEDHAZUR, E.J. (1973). *Multiple Regression in Behavioural Research*. New York: Holt, Rinehart and Winston.

KIESLING, H.J. (1969). *The Relationship of School Inputs to Public School Performance in New York State*. Santa Monica, California: Rand Corporation.

LEWIS, E.G. and MASSAD, C.E. (1975). *The Teaching of English as a Foreign Language in Ten Countries*. Stockholm: Almqvist and Wiksell.

LINDQUIST, E.F. (1966). 'Norms of achievement by schools.' In: ANASTASI, A. (Ed) *Testing Problems in Perspective*. Washington D.C.: American Council on Education.

MADAUS, G.F., AIRASIAN, P., and KELLAGHAN, T. (1971). 'The effects of standardized testing.' *Irish Journal of Education*, 5, 70–85.

MADAUS, G.F., AIRASIAN, P., and KELLAGHAN, T. (in press) *School Effectiveness*. New York: McGraw-Hill.

MADAUS, G.F., KELLAGHAN, T., and RAKOW, E. (1975). A study of the sensitivity of measures of school effectiveness. Report submitted to the Carnegie Corporation, New York. Dublin: Educational Research Centre, St. Patrick's College.

MADAUS, G.F. and LINNAN, R. (1973). 'The outcome of Catholic education?' *School Review*, 81, 207–232.

MADAUS, G.F. and MACNAMARA, J. (1969). 'Marker reliability in the Irish Leaving Certificate.' _Irish Journal of Education_, 3, 5—21.

MADAUS, G.F. and MACNAMARA, J. (1970). _Public Examinations: A study of the Irish Leaving Certificate_. Dublin: Educational Research Centre, St. Patrick's College.

MAYESKE, G.W., OKADA, T., COHEN, W.M., BEATON, A.E., and WISLER, C.E. (1973). _A Study of the Achievement of our Nation's Students_. DHEW Publication No. (OE) 72—131. Washington, D.C.: U.S. Department of Health, Education and Welfare.

MAYESKE, G.W., WISLER, C.E., BEATON, A.E., WEINFELD, F.D., COHEN, W.M., OKADA, T., PROSHEK, J.M., and TABLER, K.A. (1972). _A Study of our Nation's Schools_. DHEW Publication No. (OE) 72—142. Washington, D.C.: U.S. Department of Health, Education and Welfare.

MOLLENKOPF, W.G. and MELVILLE, S.D. (1956). A study of secondary school characteristics as related to test scores. Research Bulletin 56—6. Princeton, N.J.: Educational Testing Service.

MOOD, A.M. (1969). Macro-analysis of the American educational system. _Operations Research_, 17, 770—784.

MORRIS, N. (1961). 'An historian's view of examinations.' In: WISEMAN, S. (Ed) _Examinations and English Education_. Manchester: Manchester University Press.

MOSTELLER, F. and MOYNIHAN, D.P. (1972). 'A pathbreaking report.' In: MOSTELLER, F. and MOYNIHAN, D.P. (Eds) _On Equality of Educational Opportunity_. Papers deriving from the Harvard University faculty seminar on the Coleman report. New York: Vintage Books.

MOYNIHAN, D.P. (1968). 'Sources of resistance to the Coleman report.' _Harvard Educational Review_, 38, 23—36.

McCLELLAND, D.C. (1973). 'Testing for competence rather than for "intelligence".' _American Psychologist_, 28, 1—14.

NATIONAL ASSESSMENT OF EDUCATIONAL PROGRESS. (1974). General information yearbook. Report No. 03/04-GIY. Washington, D.C.: U.S. Government Printing Office.

NUTTALL, D.L. (1975). 'Examinations in education.' In: COX, P.R., MILES, H.B. and PEEL, J. (Eds) _Equalities and Inequalities in Education_. Proceedings of the Eleventh Annual Symposium of the Eugenics Society. London: Academic Press.

ORNSTEIN, A.C. and BERLIN, B. (1975). 'Social policy and federal funding.' _Journal of Research and Development in Education_, 8, 82—91.

PEAKER, G.F. (1967). 'The regression analyses of the national survey. Appendix 4.' In: GREAT BRITAIN: DEPARTMENT OF EDUCATION AND SCIENCE. _Children and their Primary Schools_. A report of the Central Advisory Council for Education (England). Volume II: Research and Surveys. London: Her Majesty's Stationery Office.

PIDGEON, D.A. (Ed) (1967). _Achievement in Mathematics. A national study of secondary schools_. Slough: National Foundation for Educational Research.

POREBSKI, O.R. (1966). 'On the interrelated nature of the multivariate statistics used in discriminatory analysis.' *British Journal of Mathematical and Statistical Psychology*, **19**, 197–214.

PORTER, A.C. and McDANIELS, G.L. (1974). A reassessment of the problems in estimating school effects. Paper read at 140th meeting of American Association for the Advancement of Science.

POTLETHWAITE, T.N. (1975). 'The surveys of the International Association for the Evaluation of Educational Achievement (IEA).' In: PURVES, A.C. and LEVINE, D.U. (Eds) *Educational Policy and International Assessment. Implications of the IEA surveys of achievement*. Berkeley, California: McCutchan.

PURVES, A.C. (1973). *Literature Education in Ten Countries: An empirical study*. Stockholm: Almqvist and Wiksell.

RAKOW, E.A., AIRASIAN, P.W., and MADAUS, G.F. (1978). 'Assessing school and program effectiveness: Estimating teacher level effects.' *Journal of Educational Measurement*, 15, 15–22.

RAMSØY, N.R. (1967). 'The clientele of comprehensive secondary schools in the United States.' In: ORGANISATION FOR ECONOMIC CO-OPERATION AND DEVELOPMENT: STUDY GROUP IN THE ECONOMICS OF EDUCATION AND EDUCATIONAL INVESTMENT AND PLANNING PROGRAMME. *Social objectives in educational planning*. Paris: Organisation for Economic Co-operation and Development.

RICE, J.M. (1897). 'The futility of the spelling grind.' *The Forum*, **23**, 163–172.

RIVLIN, A.M. (1971). *Systematic Thinking for Social Action*. Washington, D.C.: Brookings Institution.

ROSSI, P.H. (1972). 'Testing for success and failure in social action.' In: ROSSI, P.H. and WILLIAMS, W. (Eds) *Evaluating Social Programs. Theory, practice and politics*. New York: Seminar Press.

SACHDEVA, D. (1973). 'Estimating strength of relationship in multivariate analysis of variance.' *Educational and Psychological Measurement*, **33**, 627–631.

SMITH, M. (1972). 'Equality of educational opportunity: The basic findings reconsidered.' In: MOSTELLER, F. and MOYNIHAN, D.P. (Eds) *On Equality of Educational Opportunity*. Papers deriving from the Harvard University faculty seminar on the Coleman report. New York: Vintage Books.

SOHLMAN, A. (1971). Differences in school achievement and occupational opportunities: Explanatory factors. A survey based on European experience. In: ORGANISATION FOR ECONOMIC CO-OPERATION AND DEVELOPMENT. *Group Disparities in Educational Participation and Achievement*. Paris: Organisation for Economic Co-operation and Development.

START, K.B. and WELLS, B.K. (1972). *The Trend of Reading Standards*. Slough: National Foundation for Educational Research.

STEPHENS, J.M. (1933). *The Influence of the School upon the Individual*. Ann Arbor, Michigan: Edwards Brothers.

STEPHENS, J.M. (1967). *The Process of Schooling. A psychological examination*. New York: Holt, Rinehart and Winston.

THORNDIKE, E.L. and WOODWORTH, R.S. (1901). 'The influence of improvement in one mental function upon the efficiency of other functions.' *Psychological Review*, **8**, 247–261; 384–395; 553–564.

THORNDIKE, R.L. (1973) *Reading Comprehension Education in Fifteen Countries: An empirical study.* Stockholm: Almqvist and Wiksell.

WEISS, C.H. (1973). 'Where politics and evaluation research meet.' *Evaluation*, 1, 37—45.

WILEY, D.E. (1976). 'Another hour, another day: Quantity of schooling, a potent path for policy.' In: SEWELL, W.H., HAUSER, R.M., and FEATHERMAN, D.L. (Eds) *Schooling and Achievement in American Society.* London: Academic Press.

WILLMOTT, A.S. and NUTTALL, D.L. (1975). *The Reliability of Examinations at 16+.* Schools Council Research Studies. London: Macmillan Education.

WISEMAN, S. (1961). 'The efficiency of examinations.' In: WISEMAN, S. (Ed) *Examinations and English Education.* Manchester: Manchester University Press.

WISLER, C.E. (1974). 'Partitioning the explained variance in a regression analysis.' In: MAYESKE, G.W., BEATON, A.E., WISLER, C.E., OKADA, T., and COHEN, W.M. Technical supplement to *A Study of the Achievement of our Nation's Students.* Washington, D.C.: U.S. Department of Health, Education and Welfare.

WOOD, R. (1976). Inhibiting blind guessing: The effect of instructions. *Journal of Educational Measurement*, 13, 297—307.

WOOD, R. and WILSON, D.T. (1974). Evidence for differential marking discrimination among examiners of English. *Irish Journal of Education*, 8, 36—48.